MW01222724

本书出版得到《大中华文库》出版经费资助

大 中 华 文 库

LIBRARY OF CHINESE CLASSICS

大中华文库

汉英对照

LIBRARY OF CHINESE CLASSICS

Chinese-English

黄石公三略

THE THREE STRATEGIES OF HUANG SHIGONG

唐太宗李卫公问对

QUESTIONS AND REPLIES BETWEEN TANG TAIZONG AND LI WEIGONG

黄朴民　萧大维　校释

何小东　译

Edited and translated into modern Chinese by

Huang Pumin and Xiao Dawei

Translated into English by

He Xiaodong

军事科学出版社

Military Science Publishing House

First Edition 2004

ISBN 7-80137-720-6

Published by
Military Science Publishing House,
Academy of Military Science of
the Chinese people's Liberation Army,
Qinglongqiao, Haidian District,
Beijing 100091,China
Printed by
Shenzhen Jiaxinda Printing Co., Shenzhen, China
Printed in the People's Republic of China

总　　序

杨牧之

《大中华文库》终于出版了。我们为之高兴，为之鼓舞，但也倍感压力。

当此之际，我们愿将郁积在我们心底的话，向读者倾诉。

一

中华民族有着悠久的历史和灿烂的文化，系统、准确地将中华民族的文化经典翻译成外文，编辑出版，介绍给全世界，是几代中国人的愿望。早在几十年前，西方一位学者翻译《红楼梦》，书名译成《一个红楼上的梦》，将林黛玉译为"黑色的玉"。我们一方面对外国学者将中国的名著介绍到世界上去表示由衷的感谢，一方面为祖国的名著还不被完全认识，甚而受到曲解，而感到深深的遗憾。还有西方学者翻译《金瓶梅》，专门摘选其中自然主义描述最为突出的篇章加以译介。一时间，西方学者好像发现了奇迹，掀起了《金瓶梅》热，说中国是"性开放的源头"，公开地在报刊上鼓吹中国要"发扬开放之传统"。还有许多资深、友善的汉学家译介中国古代的哲学著作，在把中华民族文化介绍给全世界的工作方面作出了重大贡献，但或囿于理解有误，或缘于对中国文字认识的局限，质量上乘的并不多，常常是隔靴搔痒，说不到点子上。大哲学家黑格尔曾经说过：中国有最完备的国史。但他认为中国古代没有真正意义上的哲学，还处在哲学史前状态。这么了不起的哲学家竟然作出这样大失水准的评论，何其不幸。正如任何哲学家都要受时间、地点、条件的制约一样，黑格尔也离不开这一规律。当时他也只能从上述水平的汉学家译过去的文字去分析、理解，所以，黑格尔先生对中国古代社会的认识水平是什么状态，也就不难想象了。

中国离不开世界，世界也缺少不了中国。中国文化摄取外域的新成分，丰富了自己，又以自己的新成就输送给别人，贡献于世界。从公元5世纪开始到公元15世纪，大约有一千年，中国走在世界的前列。在这一千多年的时间里，她的光辉照耀全世界。人类要前进，怎么能不全面认识中国，怎么能不认真研究中国的历史呢?

二

中华民族是伟大的，曾经辉煌过，蓝天、白云、阳光灿烂，和平而兴旺；也有过黑暗的、想起来就让人战栗的日子，但中华民族从来是充满理想，不断追求，不断学习，渴望和平与友谊的。

中国古代伟大的思想家孔子曾经说过："三人行，必有我师焉。择其善者而从之，其不善者而改之。"孔子的话就是要人们向别人学习。这段话正是概括了整个中华民族与人交往的原则。人与人之间交往如此，在与周边的国家交往中也是如此。

秦始皇第一个统一了中国，可惜在位只有十几年，来不及作更多的事情。汉朝继秦而继续强大，便开始走出去，了解自己周边的世界。公元前 138 年，汉武帝派张骞出使西域。他带着一万头牛羊，总值一万万钱的金帛货物，作为礼物，开始西行，最远到过“安息”(即波斯)。公元前 36 年，班超又率 36 人出使西域。36 个人按今天的话说，也只有一个排，显然是为了拜访未曾见过面的邻居，是去交朋友。到了西域，班超派遣甘英作为使者继续西行，往更远处的大秦国(即罗马)去访问，“乃抵条支而历安息，临西海以望大秦”(《后汉书·西域传》)。“条支”在“安息”以西，即今天的伊拉克、叙利亚一带，“西海”应是今天的地中海。也就是说甘英已经到达地中海边上，与罗马帝国隔海相望，“临大海欲渡”，却被人劝阻而未成行，这在历史上留下了遗恨。可以想见班超、甘英沟通友谊的无比勇气和强烈愿望。接下来是唐代的玄奘，历经千难万险，到“西天”印度取经，带回了南亚国家的古老文化。归国后，他把带回的佛教经典组织人翻译，到后来很多经典印度失传了，但中国却保存完好，以至于今天，没有玄奘的《大唐西域记》，印度人很难编写印度古代史。明代郑和“七下西洋”，把中华文化传到东南亚一带。鸦片战争以后，一代又一代先进的中国人，为了振兴中华，又前赴后继，向西方国家学习先进的科学思想和文明成果。这中间有我们的领导人朱德、周恩来、邓小平；有许许多多大科学家、文学家、艺术家，如郭沫若、李四光、钱学森、冼星海、徐悲鸿等。他们的追求、奋斗，他们的博大胸怀，兼收并蓄的精神，为人类社会增添了光彩。

中国文化的形成和发展过程，就是一个以众为师，以各国人民为师，不断学习和创造的过程。中华民族曾经向周边国家和民族学习过许多东西，假如没有这些学习，中华民族决不可能创造出昔日的辉煌。回顾历史，我们怎么能够不对伟大的古埃及文明、古希腊文明、古印度文明满怀深深的感激?怎么能够不对伟大的欧洲文明、非洲文明、美洲文明、澳洲文明，以及中国周围的亚洲文明充满温情与敬意?

中华民族为人类社会曾作出过独特的贡献。在15世纪以前，中国的科学技术一直处于世界遥遥领先的地位。英国科学家李约瑟说:“中国在公元3世纪到13世纪之间，保持着一个西方所望尘莫及的科学知识水平。”美国耶鲁大学教授、《大国的兴衰》的作者保罗·肯尼迪坦言:“在近代以前时期的所有文明中，没有一个国家的文明比中国更发达，更先进。”

世界各国的有识之士千里迢迢来中国观光、学习。在这个过程中，中国唐朝的长安城渐渐发展成为国际大都市。西方的波斯、东罗马，东亚的高丽、新罗、百济、南天竺、北天竺，频繁前来。外国的王侯、留学生，在长安供职的外国官员，商贾、乐工和舞士，总有几十个国家，几万人之多。日本派出“遣唐使”更是一批接一批。传为美谈的日本人阿部仲麻吕(晁衡)在长安留学的故事，很能说明外国人与中国的交往。晁衡学成仕于唐朝，前后历时五十余年。晁衡与中国的知识分子结下了深厚的友情。他归国时，传说在海中遇难身亡。大诗人李白作诗哭悼:“日本晁卿辞帝都，征帆一片远蓬壶。明月不归沉碧海，白云愁色满苍梧。”晁衡遇险是误传，但由此可见中外学者之间在中国长安交往的情谊。

后来，不断有外国人到中国来探寻秘密，所见所闻，常常让他们目瞪口呆。《希腊纪事》(希腊人波桑尼阿著)记载公元2世纪时，希腊人在中国的见闻。书中写道:“赛里斯人用小米和青芦喂一种类似蜘蛛的昆虫，喂到第五年，虫肚子胀裂开，便从里面取出丝来。”从这段对中国古代养蚕技术的描述，可见当时欧洲人与中国人的差距。公元9世纪中叶，阿拉伯人来到中国。一位阿拉伯作家在他所著的《中国印度闻见录》中记载了曾旅居中国的阿拉伯商人的见闻：

——一天，一个外商去拜见驻守广州的中国官吏。会见时，外商总盯着官吏的胸部，官吏很奇怪，便问："你好像总盯着我的胸，这是怎么回事？"那位外商回答说："透过你穿的丝绸衣服，我隐约看到你胸口上长着一个黑痣，这是什么丝绸，我感到十分惊奇。"官吏听后，失声大笑，伸出胳膊，说："请你数数吧，看我穿了几件衣服？"那商人数过，竟然穿了五件之多，黑痣正是透过这五层丝绸衣服显现出来的。外商惊得目瞪口呆，官吏说："我穿的丝绸还不算是最好的，总督穿的要更精美。"

——书中关于茶(他们叫干草叶子)的记载，可见阿拉伯国家当时还没有喝茶的习惯。书中记述："中国国王本人的收入主要靠盐税和泡开水喝的一种干草税。在各个城市里，这种干草叶售价都很高，中国人称这种草叶叫'茶'，这种干草叶比苜蓿的叶子还多，也略比它香，稍有苦味，用开水冲喝，治百病。"

——他们对中国的医疗条件十分羡慕，书中记载道："中国人医疗条件很好，穷人可以从国库中得到药费。"还说："城市里，很多地方立一石碑，高10肘，上面刻有各种疾病和药物，写明某种病用某种药医治。"

——关于当时中国的京城，书中作了生动的描述：中国的京城很大，人口众多，一条宽阔的长街把全城分为两半，大街右边的东区，住着皇帝、宰相、禁军及皇家的总管、奴婢。在这个区域，沿街开凿了小河，流水潺潺；路旁，葱茏的树木整然有序，一幢幢宅邸鳞次栉比。大街左边的西区，住着庶民和商人。这里有货栈和商店，每当清晨，人们可以看到，皇室的总管、宫廷的仆役，或骑马或步行，到这里来采购。

此后的史籍对西人来华的记载，渐渐多了起来。13 世纪意大利旅行家马可·波罗，尽管有人对他是否真的到过中国持怀疑态度，但他留下一部记述元代事件的《马可·波罗游记》却是确凿无疑的。这部游记中的一些关于当时中国的描述使得西方人认为是“天方夜谭”。总之，从中西文化交流史来说，这以前的时期还是一个想象和臆测的时代，相互之间充满了好奇与幻想。

从 16 世纪末开始，由于航海技术的发展，东西方航路的开通，随着一批批传教士来华，中国与西方开始了直接的交流。沟通中西的使命在意大利传教士利玛窦那里有了充分的体现。利玛窦于 1582 年来华，1610 年病逝于北京，在华 20 余年。除了传教以外，做了两件具有历史象征意义的事，一是 1594 年前后在韶州用拉丁文翻译《四书》，并作了注释；二是与明代学者徐光启合作，用中文翻译了《几何原本》。

西方传教士对《四书》等中国经典的粗略翻译，以及杜赫德的《中华帝国志》等书对中国的介绍，在西方读者的眼前展现了一个异域文明，在当时及稍后一段时期引起了一场“中国热”，许多西方大思想家的眼光都曾注目中国文化。有的推崇中华文明，如莱布尼兹、伏尔泰、魁奈等，有的对中华文明持批评态度，如孟德斯鸠、黑格尔等。莱布尼兹认识到中国文化的某些思想与他的观念相近，如周易的卦象与他发明的二进制相契合，对中国文化给予了热情的礼赞；黑格尔则从他整个哲学体系的推演出发，认为中国没有真正意义上的哲学，还处在哲学史前的状态。但是，不论是推崇还是批评，是吸纳还是排斥，中西文化的交流产生了巨大的影响。随着先进的中国科学技术的西传，特别是中国的造纸、火药、印刷术和指南针四大发明的问世，大大改变了世界的面貌。马克思说:“中国的火药把骑士阶层炸得粉碎，指南针打开了世界市场并建立了殖民地，而印刷术则变成了新教的工具，变成对精神发展创造必要前提的最强大的杠杆。”英国的哲学家培根说：中国的四大发明“改变了全世界的面貌和一切事物的状态”。

三

大千世界，潮起潮落。云散云聚，万象更新。中国古代产生了无数伟大科学家：祖冲之、李时珍、孙思邈、张衡、沈括、毕升……，产生了无数科技成果:《齐民要术》、《九章算术》、《伤寒杂病论》、《本草纲目》……，以及保存至今的世界奇迹：浑天仪、地动仪、都江堰、敦煌石窟、大运河、万里长城……。但从 15 世纪下半叶起，风水似乎从东方转到了西方，落后的欧洲只经过 400 年便成为世界瞩目的文明中心。英国的牛顿、波兰的哥白尼、德国的伦琴、法国的居里、德国的爱因斯坦、意大利的伽利略、俄国的门捷列夫、美国的费米和爱迪生……，光芒四射，令人敬仰。

中华民族开始思考了。潮起潮落究竟是什么原因?中国人发明的火药，传到欧洲，转眼之间反成为欧洲列强轰击中国大门的炮弹，又是因为什么?

鸦片战争终于催醒了中国人沉睡的迷梦，最先“睁眼看世界”的一代精英林则徐、魏源迈出了威武雄壮的一步。曾国藩、李鸿章搞起了洋务运动。中国的知识分子喊出“民主与科学”的口号。中国是落后了，中国的志士仁人在苦苦探索。但落后中饱含着变革的动力，探索中孕育着崛起的希望。“向科学进军”，中华民族终于又迎来了科学的春天。

今天，世界毕竟来到了21世纪的门槛。分散隔绝的世界，逐渐变成联系为一体的世界。现在，全球一体化趋势日益明显，人类历史也就在愈来愈大的程度上成为全世界的历史。当今，任何一种文化的发展都离不开对其它优秀文化的汲取，都以其它优秀文化的发展为前提。在近现代，西方文化汲取中国文化，不仅是中国文化的传播，更是西方文化自身的创新和发展；正如中国文化对西方文化的汲取一样，既是西方文化在中国的传播，同时也是中国文化在近代的转型和发展。地球上所有的人类文化，都是我们共同的宝贵遗产。既然我们生活的各个大陆，在地球史上曾经是连成一气的“泛大陆”，或者说是一个完整的“地球村”，那么，我们同样可以在这个以知识和学习为特征的网络时代，走上相互学习、共同发展的大路，建设和开拓我们人类崭新的“地球村”。

西学仍在东渐，中学也将西传。各国人民的优秀文化正日益迅速地为中国文化所汲取，而无论西方和东方，也都需要从中国文化中汲取养分。正是基于这一认识，我们组织出版汉英对照版《大中华文库》，全面系统地翻译介绍中国传统文化典籍。我们试图通过《大中华文库》，向全世界展示，中华民族五千年的追求，五千年的梦想，正在新的历史时期重放光芒。中国人民就像火后的凤凰，万众一心，迎接新世纪文明的太阳。

1999年8月

PREFACE TO THE *LIBRARY OF CHINESE CLASSICS*

Yang Muzhi

The publication of the *Library of Chinese Classics* is a matter of great satisfaction to all of us who have been involved in the production of this monumental work. At the same time, we feel a weighty sense of responsibility, and take this opportunity to explain to our readers the motivation for undertaking this cross-century task.

1

The Chinese nation has a long history and a glorious culture, and it has been the aspiration of several generations of Chinese scholars to translate, edit and publish the whole corpus of the Chinese literary classics so that the nation's greatest cultural achievements can be introduced to people all over the world. There have been many translations of the Chinese classics done by foreign scholars. A few dozen years ago, a Western scholar translated the title of *A Dream of Red Mansions* into "A Dream of Red Chambers" and Lin Daiyu, the heroine in the novel, into "Black Jade." But while their endeavours have been laudable, the results of their labours have been less than satisfactory. Lack of knowledge of Chinese culture and an inadequate grasp of the Chinese written language have led the translators into many errors. As a consequence, not only are Chinese classical writings widely misunderstood in the rest of the world, in some cases their content has actually been distorted. At one time, there was a "*Jin Ping Mei* craze" among Western scholars, who thought that they had uncovered a miraculous phenomenon, and published theories claiming that China was the "fountainhead of eroticism," and that a Chinese "tradition of permissiveness" was about to be laid bare. This distorted view came about due to the translators of the *Jin Ping Mei (Plum in the Golden Vase)* putting one-sided stress on the raw elements in that novel, to the neglect of its overall literary value. Meanwhile, there have been many distinguished and well-intentioned Sinologists who have attempted to make the culture of the Chinese nation more widely known by translating works of ancient Chinese philosophy. However, the quality of such work, in many cases, is unsatisfactory, often missing the point entirely. The great philosopher Hegel considered that ancient China had no philosophy in the real sense of the word, being stuck in philosophical "prehistory." For such an eminent authority to make such a colossal error of judgment is truly regrettable. But, of course, Hegel was just as subject to the constraints of time, space and other objective conditions as anyone else, and since he had to rely for his knowledge of Chinese philosophy on inadequate translations it is not difficult to imagine why he went so far off the mark.

China cannot be separated from the rest of the world; and the rest of the world cannot ignore China. Throughout its history, Chinese civilization has enriched itself by absorbing new elements from the outside world, and in turn has contributed to the progress of world civilization as a whole by transmitting to other peoples its own cultural achievements. From the 5th to the 15th centuries, China marched in the front ranks of world civilization. If mankind wishes to advance, how can it afford to ignore China? How can it afford not to make a thoroughgoing study of its history?

2

Despite the ups and downs in their fortunes, the Chinese people have always been idealistic, and have never ceased to forge ahead and learn from others, eager to strengthen ties of peace and friendship.

The great ancient Chinese philosopher Confucius once said, "Wherever three persons come together, one of them will surely be able to teach me something. I will pick out his good points and emulate them; his bad points I will reform." Confucius meant by this that we should always be ready to learn from others. This maxim encapsulates the principle the Chinese people have always followed in their dealings with other peoples, not only on an individual basis but also at the level of state-to-state relations.

After generations of internecine strife, China was unified by Emperor

Qin Shi Huang (the First Emperor of the Qin Dynasty) in 221 B.C. The Han Dynasty, which succeeded that of the short-lived Qin, waxed powerful, and for the first time brought China into contact with the outside world. In 138 B.C., Emperor Wu dispatched Zhang Qian to the western regions, i.e. Central Asia. Zhang, who traveled as far as what is now Iran, took with him as presents for the rulers he visited on the way 10,000 head of sheep and cattle, as well as gold and silks worth a fabulous amount. In 36 B.C., Ban Chao headed a 36-man legation to the western regions. These were missions of friendship to visit neighbours the Chinese people had never met before and to learn from them. Ban Chao sent Gan Ying to explore further toward the west. According to the "Western Regions Section" in the *Book of Later Han*, Gan Ying traveled across the territories of present-day Iraq and Syria, and reached the Mediterranean Sea, an expedition which brought him within the confines of the Roman Empire. Later, during the Tang Dynasty, the monk Xuan Zang made a journey fraught with danger to reach India and seek the knowledge of that land. Upon his return, he organized a team of scholars to translate the Buddhist scriptures, which he had brought back with him. As a result, many of these scriptural classics which were later lost in India have been preserved in China. In fact, it would have been difficult for the people of India to reconstruct their own ancient history if it had not been for Xuan Zang's *A Record of a Journey to the West in the Time of the Great Tang Dynasty*. In the Ming Dynasty, Zheng He transmitted Chinese culture to Southeast Asia during his seven voyages. Following the Opium Wars in the mid-19th century, progressive Chinese, generation after generation, went to study the advanced scientific thought and cultural achievements of the Western countries. Their aim was to revive the fortunes of their own country. Among them were people who were later to become leaders of China, including Zhu De, Zhou Enlai and Deng Xiaoping. In addition, there were people who were to become leading scientists, literary figures and artists, such as Guo Moruo, Li Siguang, Qian Xuesen, Xian Xinghai and Xu Beihong. Their spirit of ambition, their struggles and their breadth of vision were an inspiration not only to the Chinese people but to people all over the world.

Indeed, it is true that if the Chinese people had not learned many things from the surrounding countries they would never have been able to produce the splendid achievements of former days. When we look back upon history, how can we not feel profoundly grateful for the legacies of the civilizations of ancient Egypt, Greece and India? How can we not feel fondness and respect for the cultures of Europe, Africa, America and Oceania?

The Chinese nation, in turn, has made unique contributions to the community of mankind. Prior to the 15th century, China led the world in science and technology. The British scientist Joseph Needham once said, "From the third century A.D. to the 13th century A.D. China was far ahead of the West in the level of its scientific knowledge." Paul Kennedy, of Yale University in the U.S., author of *The Rise and Fall of the Great Powers*, said, "Of all the civilizations of the pre-modern period, none was as well-developed or as progressive as that of China."

Foreigners who came to China were often astonished at what they saw and heard. The Greek geographer Pausanias in the second century A.D. gave the first account in the West of the technique of silk production in China: "The Chinese feed a spider-like insect with millet and reeds. After five years the insect's stomach splits open, and silk is extracted therefrom." From this extract, we can see that the Europeans at that time did not know the art of silk manufacture. In the middle of the 9th century A.D., an Arabian writer includes the following anecdote in his *Account of China and India*:

"One day, an Arabian merchant called upon the military governor of Guangzhou. Throughout the meeting, the visitor could not keep his eyes off the governor's chest. Noticing this, the latter asked the Arab merchant what he was staring at. The merchant replied, 'Through the silk robe you are wearing, I can faintly see a black mole on your chest. Your robe must be made out of very fine silk indeed!' The governor burst out laughing, and holding out his sleeve invited the merchant to count how many garments he was wearing. The merchant did so, and discovered that the governor was actually wearing five silk robes, one on top of the other, and they were made of such fine material that a tiny mole could be seen through them all! Moreover, the governor explained that the robes he was wearing were not made of the finest silk at all; silk of the highest grade was reserved for the garments worn by the provincial governor."

The references to tea in this book (the author calls it "dried grass") reveal that the custom of drinking tea was unknown in the Arab countries at that time: "The king of China's revenue comes mainly from taxes on salt and the dry leaves of a kind of grass which is drunk after boiled water is poured on it. This dried grass is sold at a high price in every city in the country. The Chinese call it 'cha.' The bush is like alfalfa, except that it bears more leaves, which are also more fragrant than alfalfa. It has a slightly bitter taste, and when it is infused in boiling water it is said to have medicinal properties."

Foreign visitors showed especial admiration for Chinese medicine. One wrote, "China has very good medical conditions. Poor people are given money to buy medicines by the government."

In this period, when Chinese culture was in full bloom, scholars flocked from all over the world to China for sightseeing and for study. Chang'an, the capital of the Tang Dynasty was host to visitors from as far away as the Byzantine Empire, not to mention the neighboring countries of Asia. Chang'an, at that time the world's greatest metropolis, was packed with thousands of foreign dignitaries, students, diplomats, merchants, artisans and entertainers. Japan especially sent contingent after contingent of envoys to the Tang court. Worthy of note are the accounts of life in Chang'an written by Abeno Nakamaro, a Japanese scholar who studied in China and had close friendships with ministers of the Tang court and many Chinese scholars in a period of over 50 years. The description throws light on the exchanges between Chinese and foreigners in this period. When Abeno was supposedly lost at sea on his way back home, the leading poet of the time, Li Bai, wrote a eulogy for him.

The following centuries saw a steady increase in the accounts of China written by Western visitors. The Italian Marco Polo described conditions in China during the Yuan Dynasty in his *Travels*. However, until advances in the science of navigation led to the opening of east-west shipping routes at the beginning of the 16th century Sino-Western cultural exchanges were coloured by fantasy and conjecture. Concrete progress was made when a contingent of religious missionaries, men well versed in Western science and technology, made their way to China, ushering in an era of direct contacts between China and the West. The experience of this era was embodied in the career of the Italian Jesuit Matteo Ricci. Arriving in China in 1582, Ricci died in Beijing in 1610. Apart from his missionary work, Ricci accomplished two historically symbolic tasks — one was the translation into Latin of the "Four Books," together with annotations, in 1594; the other was the translation into Chinese of Euclid's *Elements*.

The rough translations of the "Four Books" and other Chinese classical works by Western missionaries, and the publication of Père du Halde's *Description Geographique, Historique, Chronologique, Politique, et Physique de l'Empire de la Chine* revealed an exotic culture to Western readers, and sparked a "China fever," during which the eyes of many Western intellectuals were fixed on China. Some of these intellectuals, including Leibniz, held China in high esteem; others, such as Hegel, nursed a critical attitude toward Chinese culture. Leibniz considered that some aspects of Chinese thought were close to his own views, such as the philosophy of the *Book of Changes* and his own binary system. Hegel, on the other hand, as mentioned above, considered that China had developed no proper philosophy of its own. Nevertheless, no matter whether the reaction was one of admiration, criticism, acceptance or rejection, Sino-Western exchanges were of great significance. The transmission of advanced Chinese science and technology to the West, especially the Chinese inventions of paper-making, gunpowder, printing and the compass, greatly changed the face of the whole world. Karl Marx said, "Chinese gunpowder blew the feudal class of knights to smithereens; the compass opened up world markets and built colonies; and printing became an implement of Protestantism and the most powerful lever and necessary precondition for intellectual development and creation." The English philosopher Roger Bacon said that China's four great inventions had "changed the face of the whole world and the state of affairs of everything."

3

Ancient China gave birth to a large number of eminent scientists, such as Zu Chongzhi, Li Shizhen, Sun Simiao, Zhang Heng, Shen Kuo and Bi

Sheng. They produced numerous treatises on scientific subjects, including *The Manual of Important Arts for the People's Welfare, Nine Chapters on the Mathematical Art, A Treatise on Febrile Diseases* and *Compendium of Materia Medica.* Their accomplishments included ones whose influence has been felt right down to modern times, such as the armillary sphere, seismograph, Dujiangyan water conservancy project, Dunhuang Grottoes, Grand Canal and Great Wall. But from the latter part of the 15th century, and for the next 400 years, Europe gradually became the cultural centre upon which the world's eyes were fixed. The world's most outstanding scientists then were England's Isaac Newton, Poland's Copernicus, France's Marie Curie, Germany's Rontgen and Einstein, Italy's Galileo, Russia's Mendelev and America's Edison.

The Chinese people then began to think: What is the cause of the rise and fall of nations? Moreover, how did it happen that gunpowder, invented in China and transmitted to the West, in no time at all made Europe powerful enough to batter down the gates of China herself?

It took the Opium War to wake China from its reverie. The first generation to make the bold step of "turning our eyes once again to the rest of the world" was represented by Lin Zexu and Wei Yuan. Zeng Guofan and Li Hongzhang started the Westernization Movement, and later intellectuals raised the slogan of "Democracy and Science." Noble-minded patriots, realizing that China had fallen behind in the race for modernization, set out on a painful quest. But in backwardness lay the motivation for change, and the quest produced the embryo of a towering hope, and the Chinese people finally gathered under a banner proclaiming a "March Toward Science."

On the threshold of the 21st century, the world is moving in the direction of becoming an integrated entity. This trend is becoming clearer by the day. In fact, the history of the various peoples of the world is also becoming the history of mankind as a whole. Today, it is impossible for any nation's culture to develop without absorbing the excellent aspects of the cultures of other peoples. When Western culture absorbs aspects of Chinese culture, this is not just because it has come into contact with Chinese culture, but also because of the active creativity and development of Western culture itself; and vice versa. The various cultures of the world's peoples are a precious heritage which we all share. Mankind no longer lives on different continents, but on one big continent, or in a "global village." And so, in this era characterized by an all-encompassing network of knowledge and information we should learn from each other and march in step along the highway of development to construct a brand-new "global village."

Western learning is still being transmitted to the East, and vice versa. China is accelerating its pace of absorption of the best parts of the cultures of other countries, and there is no doubt that both the West and the East need the nourishment of Chinese culture. Based on this recognition, we have edited and published the *Library of Chinese Classics* in a Chinese-English format as an introduction to the corpus of traditional Chinese culture in a comprehensive and systematic translation. Through this collection, our aim is to reveal to the world the aspirations and dreams of the Chinese people over the past 5,000 years and the splendour of the new historical era in China. Like a phoenix rising from the ashes, the Chinese people in unison are welcoming the cultural sunrise of the new century.

August 1999

《黄石公三略》简介

《黄石公三略》，中国古代著名兵书，"武经七书"之一。亦称《三略》，分上、中、下 3 卷，约 3800 余字。

关于本书作者和成书时代，向来是兵书研究中的一大谜团。《隋书·经籍志》著录"《黄石公三略》3 卷，下邳神人撰"。所谓下邳神人，就是那位授张良以兵书的著名隐士黄石公，时间当在秦汉间。然此说疑点颇多，难以成立。军事史学者黄朴民先生认为，此书当产生于东汉末年，作者已不可详考。

本书最显著的思想特色是兼容博采，集中反映了东汉末年的社会思潮，在一定程度上体现了中国古代兵学演变递嬗的基本轨迹。《三略》以道家最高哲学范畴——道，统摄全书，师古而不泥古，在继承前代兵学理论的基础上，主张以道家谋略取天下，以儒家思想安天下，以法家原则御将卒，以阴阳家观点识形势，以墨家的人才观尚贤纳士。杂取诸家之长而又相辅相成，形成浑然一体且又独具特色的兵学思想体系。其中侧重从国家大战略的角度考察军事问题，注重论述治军御将而淡化申说作战指导，是《三略》一书的显著特点。

此书唐代传到日本，开始走向世界。

此次整理时，《三略》原文以宋版《武经七书》本为底本，并注意吸收前人及当代学者的核勘整理成果，择其善者而从之。对底本中明显的讹夺之处，径将改补文字以圆括孤置于文中，对常见的通假字、异体字，亦是径改未注。现代汉语释文，以军事科学出版社《武经七书鉴赏》（2002版）为底本，并参以解放军出版社的《武经七书注译》（1986年版）、《黄石公三略浅说》

（1987 年版）等书。英文译文参考了拉尔夫•索耶翻译，西景出版社出版的《武经七书》（1993 年版）。限于体例，以上诸点，书中未能详加说明。读者见谅。

王显臣

An Introduction to *Three Strategies of Huang Shigong*

The *Three Strategies of Huang Shigong* is a renowned ancient Chinese military book and one of the Seven Military Classics of Ancient China. It is also called the *Three Strategies,* consisting of the three books of *Superior Strategy, Middle Strategy* and *Inferior Strategy,* totaling about 3800 words.

Its author and the year it was written has long been a big mystery in the study of military classics. The "Bibliography *of* Classics" in *the Sui Book* lists all three books of the *Three Strategies of Huang Shigong* attributing their authorship to "a genius from the prefecture of Xia Pi." This so-called genius from prefecture of Xiapi was said to be the well-known hermit Huang Shigong who was said to have given a book on the art of war to the military strategist Zhang Liang during the years between the Qin and Han dynasties. There are, however, quite a few questionable points about this assertion, therefore making it hardly tenable. According to the military historian Mr. Huang Pumin, this book should be written in the late years of the Eastern Han Dynasty and the author is unable to be verified.

The most prominent conceptual character of this book is that, by extensively absorbing and collecting various materials, it reflects the trends of thought of the late years of the Eastern Han Dynasty and indicates, to some extent, the basic path of development of ancient Chinese theories of war. The *Three Strategies* is permeated with *Dao(Tao),* or Right Way, the tiptop Daoist (Taoist) philosophical concept. It learns from the past but is not confined thereto. While having inherited the military theories and concepts of earlier ages, it advocates to take the world with Taoist strategies, to pacify the world with Confucian thinking, to command the armed forces with Legalist doctrines, to analyze the situation from the viewpoints of the *Yin–Yang* School and to recruit worthies in line with the Mohist conception of talents. It learns from merits of all schools and makes them mutually supplementary each other to become an integrated system of military thoughts with its own characteristics, of which, the most notable is that it stresses studying military issues from the angle of the nation's overall strategy and focusing on how to command and control the generals and troops while purposely toning down the education of combat tactics.

The book found its way to Japan during the Tang Dynasty, thenceforth to the rest of the world.

For this edition, the text of *the Three Strategies of Huang Shigong* is based on *The Seven Military*

Classics of the Song Dynasty (960-1279) edition, and we have drawn upon the textual research and collation of contemporary scholars and their predecessors, incorporating their achievements and insights. Corrected and added Chinese characters are enclosed in parentheses where there exist obvious errors and gaps in the original classical Chinese text, while the classical variations of some Chinese characters are not corrected or explained with notes. The text is translated into modern Chinese based on *Understanding the Seven Military Classics* (2002) published by the Military Science Publishing House and with *The Seven Military Classics with Notes and Translation* (1986) and *Introduction to the Three Strategies of Huang Shigong* (1987), published by the People's Liberation Army Press, as the reference books. The text is translated into English with The *Seven Military Classics of Ancient China* (1993) translated by Ralph D. Sawyer and published by the Westview Press as the reference book. The references are not required by the stylistic rules of this edition to be noted one by one,and we request the understanding of the readers.

By Wang Xianchen

《唐太宗李卫公问对》简介

《唐太宗李卫公问对》，又称《唐李问对》、《李卫公问对》、《李靖问对》，简称《问对》。中国古代著名兵书，“武经七书”之一。分上中下三卷，万余言。

本书以唐太宗李世民与卫国公李靖讨论兵法形式写成。书未必是唐李亲著，当是君臣论兵言论辑录，经后人整理成书，反映了唐初二位军事家的军事思想。在中国兵学史上占有重要一席，对后世影响深远。

本书对中国传统兵学进行了一次系统总结，有关兵学源流、范畴术语、战略得失、阵法考辨、军制沿革、治军要则、用人机宜、战法战例，均能纵论古今，正本清源，使得“兵家术法，灿然毕举，皆可垂范将来”。

本书多有创新之见。自《孙子》以降，“奇正”、“虚实”、“主客”、“攻守”等兵家术语，沿用成习，内涵稳定。《问对》不拘成说，开掘深蕴，创立新意，指出，关键在于争取战场主动权，“千章万句，不出乎‘致人而不致于人’而已”。使人耳目一新，思路大开。

结合实例评点古人得失，讨论兵学旨要，是本书的又一特点。武王伐纣、淝水之战、霍邑之战、黄帝兵法、《曹公新书》、武侯八阵，井田兵制，考索析疑，论辩短长，在平实亲切中，见人所未见，道人所未明。

另外，《问对》一书重视部队的教育训练与管理，重视官兵关系，反对以占验卜筮等迷信活动决策军事行动，坚持唯物思想。在这些问题上，都有深刻的见地和论述，很值得后世治军者借鉴。

此次整理时，《问对》原文以宋版《武经七书》本为底本，并注意吸收前人及当代学者的核勘整理成果，择其善者而从之。对底本中明显的讹夺之处，径将改补文字以圆括孤置于文中，对常见的通假字、异体字，亦是径改未注。现代汉语释文，以军事科学出版社《武经七书鉴赏》（2002 版）为底本，并参以解放军出版社的《武经七书注译》（1986 年版）、《唐太宗李卫公问对浅说》（1987 年版）等书。英文译文参考了拉尔夫•索耶翻译，西景出版社出版的《武经七书》（1993 年版）。限于体例，以上诸点，书中未能详加说明。读者见谅。

王显臣

An Introduction to *Questions and Replies between Tang Taizong and Li Weigong*

The *Questions and Replies between Tang Taizong and Li Weigong,* also called *Questions and Replies between Tang and Li, Questions and Replies by Li Weigong, Replies by Li Jing, or Questions and Replies* for short, is a renowned ancient Chinese military book and one of the Seven Military Classics of Ancient China, consisting of three chapters totaling about ten thousand words.

The book is written in a style of questions and replies between Tang Taizong (Li Shiming, or Enperor Tai Zong of the Tang Dynasty) and the Duke of Wei Li Jing on the art of war. It might not have been written by Tang and Li themselves but very possibly is a verbatim record of the discourses between the monarch and his courtier on military affairs, compiled by people of later generations into a book reflecting the military thinking of the two strategists in the early Tang Dynasty. The book has a notable niche in the history of Chinese military science and exerts a significant influence on posterity.

The book is a systematic summary of traditional Chinese military theories. Touching upon topics such as sources of military theory, conceptual terminology, strategic gains and losses, battle formations, evolution of military organizations, main principles of running an army, ways of selecting and employing right people, military tactics, and cases of speific battles, it makes critical remarks on people or things past and present and tackles the problems at their roots, "making the tactics and techniques of famous military strategists all come forth as brilliant examples for posterity," as a critic once put it.

The book contains many innovative ideas and visions. Since *Sun Zi' Art of War* was brought forth, such military terms as "orthodox and unorthodox," "strengths and weakness," "host and guest" and "offense and defense" have been used as common expressions with rather stabilized meanings. *Questions and Replies,* nevertheless, does not confine itself to established formulations but tries to provide new insights and give some innovative explanations. It points out that what is most important is to seize the initiative in the battlefield, and that "there are thousands of articles and tens of thousands of words about military strategy and tactics, but none of them will go beyond the principle of 'bringing the enemy to battle and not being brought there by him'," Statements like these really bear something fresh and new and broadens people's vision.

Another characteristic of this book is that it makes comments on the gains and losses of the ancients and discusses the essences of the art of war on the basis of past examples — the expedition of King Wu of Zhou against King Zhou of Shang, the Battle of Fei Shui, the Battle of Huo Yi, the art of war of the Yellow Emperor, the *New Book of Duke Cao,* the Eight Formations of Marquis Wu, the Nine Square System, etc. It verifies facts and clears doubts, comments on merits and argues about demerits, and in a very simple and plain manner looks into something never before looked into and clarifies something never before clarified.

Furthermore, *Questions and Replies* pays great attention to the education, training and administration of the troops, lays stress on the relationship between officers and soldiers, objects to relying on superstition and divination to decide military operations, and holds firmly to materialism. Its viewpoints and comments on these issues are all very profound and worth learning by the military teaders of later generations.

For this edition, the text of *Questions and Replies between Tang Taizong and Li Weigong* is based on *The Seven Military Classics* of the Song Dynasty (960-1279) edition, and we have drawn upon the textual research and collation of contemporary scholars and their predecessors, incorporating their achievements and insights. Corrected and added Chinese characters are enclosed in parentheses where there exist obvious errors and gaps in the original classical Chinese text, while the classical variations of some Chinese characters are not corrected or explained with notes. The text is translated into modern Chinese based on *Understanding the Seven Military Classics* (2002) published by the Military Science Publishing House and with *The Seven Military Classics with Notes and Translation* (1986) and *Introduction to Questions and Replies between Tang Taizong and Li Weigong* (1987), published by the People's Liberation Army Press, as the reference books. The text is translated into English with The *Seven Military Classics of Ancient China* (1993) translated by Ralph D. Sawyer and published by the Westview Press as the reference book.The references are not required by the stylistic rules of this edition to be noted one by one, and we request the understanding of the readers.

By Wan Xianchen

目　录

CONTENTS

黄石公三略

THE THREE STRATEGIES OF HUANG SHIGONG

卷上

上略

【原文】

夫主将之法，务揽英雄之心，赏禄有功，通志于众。故与众同好靡不成，与众同恶靡不倾。治国安家，得人也；亡国破家，失人也。含气之类，咸愿得其志。

《军谶》曰：“柔能制刚，弱能制强。”柔者，德也；刚者，贼也。弱者人之所助，强者怨之所攻。

【今译】

统帅将领的方法，务必收揽英雄豪杰的心，将禄位赏赐给有功之臣，使自己的意志成为众人共同的意志。所以，与大家有共同的意愿，就没有做不成的事情；与大家有共同的仇恨，就没有打不垮的敌人。国家大治，家庭安好，是由于获得了人心；国家覆灭，家庭破亡，是由于丧失了人心。因为所有的人都愿意实现自己的志向。

《军谶》上说：“柔的能够制服刚的，弱的能够制服强的。”柔而得当是美德，刚而不当是灾祸。弱小的一方，往往容易得到别人的帮助；强大的一方，则常常会成为招致怨恨和攻击的目标。柔有柔的用

BOOK I

SUPERIOR STRATEGY

To command the generals, you must first win the minds of the men of valor and character, reward and provide salaries to the meritorious, and let your own will become the will of the masses. Thus if you have the same wishes as the masses, there is nothing you will not accomplish. If you have the same hatred as the masses, there is no enemy you will not defeat. If the state is in great order and peace and the families are safe and sound, it is because you have gained the hearts of the people, while if the state is in ruin and the families are destroyed, it is because you have lost the hearts of the people. Everyone would like to realize his ambitions.

The Military Prophecies states: "The mild can overcome the tough, the weak can overcome the strong." Proper mildness is virtue, improper

【原文】

柔有所设，刚有所施，弱有所用，强有所加。兼此四者而制其宜。

端末未见，人莫能知。天地神明，与物推移，变动无常。因敌转化，不为事先，动而辄随。故能图制无疆，扶成天威，匡正八极，密定九夷。如此谋者，为帝王师。

故曰：莫不贪强，鲜能守微，若能守微，乃保

【今译】

处，刚有刚的作用，弱有弱的意义，强有强的地位，应该把这四者有机地结合起来，因事制宜地加以运用。

事物的始末没有显现，人们就不能认识它。大自然神奇莫测，随着事物的运动而推移，变化无常。根据敌情的变化而行动，即不要首先发难，而是要随着敌人的行动采取相应适宜的对策。这样就能够图谋制胜，无往而不利，辅佐君王树立天威，匡正天下，安定边远地区。这样运筹谋划的人，可以成为帝王的老师。

所以说，凡人没有不贪强好胜的，但很少有人能把握以柔弱制服刚强这一幽深精微的道理。如果能掌握这个精微的奥秘，便可以保全自己的事业和生命。圣人掌握了这一幽深精微的道理，所以行动

toughness leads to disaster. Those who are weak tend to win support from the others, while those who are strong tend to bring about resentment and be attacked. There are situations where mildness has its uses, toughness has its role to play, weakness has its significance and strength has its positions. These four should be combined appropriately and employed in line with the varied situations.

You can not know a thing when neither its beginning nor its end has yet become visible. Nature is mystical and unfathomable and transforms and changes constantly with the movement of things. One should move and act in response to the enemy, that is, should not initiate an attack but take appropriate measures in accordance with the enemy's movement. Thus one is able to formulate inexhaustible strategies and be ever-victorious, is able to assist to sustain and complete the awe-inspiring power of the sovereign, correct the maladies, bring tranquility and order to the country and settle the remote areas. Such a strategist can be a teacher for an emperor or a king.

Thus it is said that everyone covets strength

【原文】

其生。圣人存之，动应事机。舒之弥四海，卷之不盈怀，居之不以室宅，守之不以城廓，藏之胸臆，而敌国服。

《军谶》曰："能柔能刚，其国弥光；能弱能强，其国弥彰。纯柔纯弱，其国必削；纯刚纯强，其国必亡。"

夫为国之道，恃贤与民。信贤如腹心，使民如

【今译】

起来就能顺应事物的规律。推行开来可以遍布于天下，收拢起来可以不出乎寸心。安放它不必用上房屋，守护它无须依靠城廓。只要收藏于胸中加以巧妙的运用，就可以迫使敌国屈服。

《军谶》上说："既能用柔，又能用刚，国家的前途就充满光明；既能用弱，又能用强，国家的形势就更加昌盛。单纯用柔或单纯用弱，国家就必然遭到削弱；单纯用刚或单纯用强，国家就注定走向灭亡。"

治理国家的原则，是依赖贤士和民众。信任贤士如同自己的心腹，使用民众如同自己的四肢，那

and likes to outdo others, but rare are those capable of understanding the subtle idea that the mild can overcome the tough. If one understands that subtle idea, his life and course can be protected and preserved. The Sage understands it, so he acts and moves all in response to the laws and changes of things. He can spread it all over the world and he can roll it up in his heart. He does not need a house to settle it down and he does not need city walls to protect it. Provided that he has it in his mind and applies it cleverly, the enemy state will submit.

The Military Prophecies states: "To be not only able to be mild but also tough, the state will have a bright future; to be not only able to be weak but also strong, the state will become increasingly prosperous; to be merely mild or weak, the state will inevitably decline and to be merely tough or strong, the state will be doomed to perish."

The way to govern a state is to rely on virtuous and wise persons and the ordinary people. If you trust virtuous and wise persons as if they were your heart and belly and employ the ordinary people as if they were your limbs, then all

【原文】

四肢，则策无遗。所适如支体相随，骨节相救，天道自然，其巧无间。

军国之要，察众心，施百务。危者安之，惧之欢之，叛者还之，冤者原之，诉者察之，卑者贵之，强者抑之，敌者残之，贪者丰之，欲者使之，畏者隐之，谋者近之，谗者覆之，毁者复之，反者废之，横者挫之，满者损之，归者招之，服者居之，降者

【今译】

么政令就不会有纰漏，行动起来就会像四肢与躯干一样的协调，骨节之间互相照应，浑然天成，巧妙无间。

治国统军的要旨，在于体察民众的思想感情，采取各种妥善的措施。处境危险的要使他平安无事，心怀忧惧的要使他欢愉高兴，背叛逃亡的要使他重新归来，含冤受屈的要予以昭雪平反，上告申诉的要为他调查清楚，地位卑贱的要使他变得尊贵，强横不法的要加以抑制，与我为敌的要使他遭到毁灭，贪婪爱财的就多给财物，愿意效力的就加以任用，怕人揭短的就予以隐讳，对有智谋韬略的人要多多同他亲近，对爱进谗言的人不要予以信任，对毁谤者的话要反复进行核实，谋反作乱的要予以铲除，强梁暴虐的要让他受挫，骄傲自满的要给予抑制，倾心归顺的要给予招抚，已被征服的要给予安置，

your policies and orders will be well followed and accomplished and your move will be in very good harmony, just as natural and wonderful as the limbs coordinating with the body and the joints of the bones with each other.

The essence of governing a state and commanding an army is to be aware of what the people think and feel and take various measures accordingly; to make those who are in danger safe and those who are sad and afraid happy; to have those who have rebelled and fled come back; to rehabilitate the misjudged and investigate for those who have legal suits; to raise up the lowly and repress those who are brutal and out of laws; to destroy those who are hostile and enrich those who are greedy; to use those who desire to serve; to conceal the secret for those who have some weaknesses and faults; to stay close to those who are wise and strategists; to distrust those who like to make false accusations and investigate and verify the slanders; to eliminate the rebellious and stifle those who act willfully; to diminish the arrogant and summon those who turn their allegiance toward you; to settle down those who have been conquered and be benevo-

【原文】

脱之。

获固守之，获厄塞之，获难屯之，获城割之，获地裂之，获财散之。

敌动伺之，敌近备之，敌强下之，敌佚去之，敌陵待之，敌暴绥之，敌悖义之，敌睦携之，顺举挫之，因势破之，放言过之，四网罗之。

得而勿有，居而勿守，拔而勿久，立而勿取，

【今译】

已经投降的要加以宽恕。

占领了坚固的地方要加以守备，占领了险隘的地方要加以阻塞，攻取了不容易得到的地方要驻兵屯守，攻取了城邑要分赏有功之臣，得到土地要裂土分封，得到财物要散发给众人。

敌人行动要密切地加以监视，敌人逼近要严密地加以防备，敌人强大要故意向它示弱，敌军以逸待劳要注意避其兵锋，敌人来犯要严阵以待，敌人暴虐我就要安抚民众，敌人悖逆我就要伸张正义，敌人和睦团结就要设法进行分化离间。要顺应敌人的行动去挫败它，要利用敌人的情势去击破它，散布假情报诱使敌人发生错误，四面包围敌人将其一举歼灭。

取得胜利不要归功于自己名下，取得财物不要自己专有享受，攻取城池不要旷日持久，拥立他人为君而自己不要去当，决策出自于自己，功劳归之

lent toward the surrendered.

If you take a strong point, defend it. If you take a defile, block it. If you take a terrain which is difficult to take, then deploy troops to hold it. If you secure a city, grant it to those who have done meritorious service. If you seize a territory, divide it up to enfeoff the nobles. If you obtain wealth, distribute it to the troops.

When the enemy moves, observe him closely; when he approaches, get well prepared for him. If the enemy is strong, make him believe that you are weak. If the enemy is well rested, avoid his forceful part. If the enemy assaults, wait in full battle array. If the enemy is brutal, then show more love toward the people. If the enemy is immoral, then uphold justice. If the enemy is harmonious and united, try to split and demoralize him. Initiate measures and repress the enemy in accordance with his actions, defeat him in accordance with the situation, spread false information and cause him to make mistakes and siege him and wipe him out at one go.

When you win, do not attribute the victory to yourself; when you gain wealth, do not keep it for yourself; when you try to seize a city, do not prolong the attack. Designate a new ruler but do

【原文】

为者则己，有者则士，焉知利之所在！彼为诸侯，己为天子，使城自保，令士自取。

世能祖祖，鲜能下下。祖祖为亲，下下为君。下下者，务耕桑不夺其时，簿（薄）赋敛不匮其财，罕傜役不使其劳，则国富而家娭，然后选士以司牧之。夫所谓士者，英雄也。故曰：罗其英雄，

【今译】

于将士，须知道这才是真正的利益之所在啊！别人都是诸侯，自己才是天子，让各个城邑自我保护，让官吏贤士自行征收各种赋税。

世上的君主都能尊崇自己的祖先，但很少有人能爱护、体贴那些地位卑微的民众。礼敬祖先只是亲情之道，爱抚民众才是为君之道。爱抚民众，就是要重视耕作蚕织，不侵占农时，减轻赋税，不使民众贫困匮乏；减少傜役，不使民众劳困疲敝。这样，便可以做到国家富足，家庭安乐，然后再选择贤士去管理他们。所谓贤士，就是那些英雄豪杰。所以说，能够罗致敌国的英雄豪杰，就可以使敌国

not make yourself the ruler. Make decisions yourself but give credit to the officers and soldiers and this is where the real profit lies. All the others are only feudal lords and you are the emperor, the Son of Heaven. Let the cities defend themselves and let the officials and worthies collect the taxes and levies.

Most of the monarchs in the world venerate their ancestors, but few of them think and care for the humble people. To venerate the ancestors is the way to show familial emotional connections while to care for the people is the way to be a ruler. To take good care of the people means concentrating on agriculture and sericulture and not disturbing them during their vital seasonal occupations. It means to reduce the taxes and levies, not to exhaust their wealth, not to impose too much conscript labor, and not to cause them to be overly labored. Thus the state will be prosperous and the families will live in peace and contentment. Only thereafter should you select worthy persons to control and supervise them. What are termed worthy persons are men of character and valor. So if you can draw

【原文】

则敌国穷。英雄者，国之干；庶民者，国之本。得其干，收其本，则政行而无怨。

夫用兵之要，在崇礼而重禄。礼崇则智士至，禄重则义士轻死。故禄贤不爱财，赏功不逾时，则下力并而敌国削。夫用人之道，尊以爵，赡以财，则士自来；接以礼，励以义，则士死之。

夫将帅者，必与士卒同滋味而共安危，敌乃可加，故兵有全胜，敌有全因（囚）。昔者良将之用

【今译】

陷于困窘的境地。英雄豪杰，是国家的骨干；普通民众，是国家的根本。获得了骨干，掌握了根本，就能够做到政令畅通而民众毫无埋怨。

用兵打仗的要义，在于崇尚礼节和厚施俸禄。崇尚礼节，那么智谋之士就会归附；厚施俸禄，那么侠义之士就会乐于效死。因此，优待贤士不要吝惜财物，奖赏功臣不要拖延时日，这样就能够使部下齐心协力而削弱敌国。任贤用人的方法，是通过封赐爵位来尊崇他，给予财物以赡养他。如此，贤士就会自愿来归；用礼仪来接待他，用道义来激励他，如此，贤士就会以死相报。

身为将帅的，必须和士卒同甘苦而共安危，这样才可以与敌人进行交锋，所以战争必将取得彻底胜利，敌人必将完全覆灭。从前优秀的将帅用兵打

in men of character and valor from an enemy state, then the enemy state will fall into an awkward predicament. Men of character and valor are the backbone of a state, while ordinary people are its root. If you have the backbone and secure the root, government decrees will be implemented without resentment.

What is essential in employing and commanding troops is to treat your men with courtesy and provide them with a good salary. To be courteous, wise men will turn their allegiance toward you; with good salaries, gallant men will be happy to die for you. So, do not be grudging in treating the worthy and do not hesitate in awarding the meritorious, thus your men will work as one and the enemy state will be weakened. The way to employ worthies is to respect them by awarding them noble ranks and supply them with material goods, then the worthies will come of their own accord. Welcome them with courtesy and stimulate them with righteousness, and they will die for you.

To be a commanding general, you must share comforts and hardships with your men and confront safety and danger together with them, for

【原文】

兵，有馈箪醪者，使投诸河，与士卒同流而饮。夫一箪之醪不能味一河之水，而三军之士思为致死者，以滋味之及己也。《军谶》曰："军井未达，将不言渴；军幕未办，将不言倦；军灶未炊，将不言饥。冬不服裘，夏不操扇，雨不张盖，是谓将礼。与之安，与之危，故其众可合而不可离，可用而不可疲，

【今译】

仗，有人赠送给他一坛美酒，他让人把美酒统统倾倒在河中，并与士兵们同饮河水。一坛酒并不能使一河之水都有酒味，而三军将士却都愿意为将帅拼死效力，这是因为将帅与自己同甘共苦的缘故。《军谶》上说："军井还没有凿成，将帅不说口渴；军帐还没有搭好，将帅不说疲乏；军灶还没有做好，将帅不说饥饿。冬天不穿皮衣，夏天不用扇子，雨天不独自打伞，这就是做将帅的基本要求。与士卒们同安乐，与士卒们共危难，所以，全军上下能齐心协力而不可分离，能够任意使用而不知疲倦，这

then you will be able to engage the enemy, win a full victory and defeat the enemy completely. In antiquity, there was a case where an outstanding general at war was presented with a cask of good wine. The general had it poured into the river and drank the water of the river with his men. A cask of wine is unable to flavor a river of water, but the officers and soldiers of his army were all motivated and eager to fight to their death because their commanding general shared weal and woe with them. *The Military Prophecies states:* "When the army's wells have not yet been completed, the general does not mention thirst. When the encampment has not yet been set up, the general does not speak about fatigue. When the army's cookstoves have not yet been lit, the general does not speak about hunger. In winter he does not wear a fur robe; in summer he does not use a fan; and in rain he does not set up an umbrella. These are the basic requirements for a commanding general. Share comforts and happiness with the men and confront hardships and danger together with them, and the men will work as one and never be forced apart, will be employed at will and never be tired out. All this comes from the favors and rewards

【原文】

以其恩素蓄，谋素和也。”故曰：蓄恩不倦，以一取万。《军谶》曰：“将之所以为威者，号令也；战之所以全胜者，军政也；士之所以轻战者，用命也。”故将无还令，赏罚必信；如天如地，乃可御人；士卒用命，乃可越境。

夫统军持势者，将也；制胜破敌者，众也。故乱将不可使保军，乖众不可使伐人。攻城则不拔，

【今译】

正是因为平时恩惠有加、思想一致的缘故。所以说，将帅不断地施加恩惠于广大士卒，就能够赢得千千万万人的拥戴。《军谶》上说：“将帅之所以有威严，是由于号令严明；作战之所以取得全胜，是因为军政整饬；士卒之所以不惧怕打仗，是由于听从命令。”所以，将帅一旦发布命令，就不可以再收回，赏罚一定要严守信用，像天地一样不可移易，这样才可以统御大军；兵士拼死效命，这样才可以出境作战。

统领军队控制局势的是将帅，战胜敌人夺取胜利的是兵众。所以，治军无方的将领不能让他去统率军队，离心离德的军队不能用来攻伐敌人。（这

granted routinely and the consistence in thinking gained daily." Thus it is said that if a commanding general keeps granting favors and rewards to his men, he will enjoy support from tens of thousands of people."

The Military Prophecies states: "The awesomeness of the general depends on the strictness of his commands and orders; a total victory of a battle depends on the military management and administration. The reason why the troops do not fear to fight is that they submit themselves to orders and commands." Thus a commanding general never rescinds an order once it is given. Rewards and punishments must be as certain and convincing as Heaven and Earth, for then the general is able to command a great army and his men will go all out at the risk of their lives and the army can fight a war across the border.

It is the generals who command the army and control the situation. It is the troops who defeat the enemy and win the war. Thus an incompetent general should not be employed to command the army while rebellious and dissonant

【原文】

图邑则不废，二者无功，则士力疲弊。士力疲弊，则将孤众悖，以守则不固，以战则奔北，是谓老兵。兵老则将威不行，将无威则士卒轻刑，士卒轻刑则军失伍，军失伍则士卒逃亡，士卒逃亡则敌乘利，敌乘利则军必丧。

《军谶》曰："良将之统军也，恕（恕）己而治

【今译】

样的军队）若是去攻打城池则不能拔取，图谋市镇则难以占领，攻城图邑这两者都劳而无功，那么军力就会疲惫不堪。军力疲惫不堪，那么将领就会陷于孤立，士卒就会悖逆抗命，用来守御则不稳固，用来作战则溃散败逃，这就叫做师老兵疲。师老兵疲，那么将领的威严就会丧失；将领没有威严，那么士卒就会不畏惧刑罚；士卒不畏惧刑罚，那么军队就会发生混乱；军队发生混乱，那么士卒就会逃亡；士卒逃亡，那么敌人就会趁机取利；敌人趁机取利，那么军队就必定走向败亡。

《军谶》上说："优秀的将领统率军队，总是以

troops should not be used to attack the enemy. If such an army is used to attack a city, the city will not be taken while if it is used to lay siege to a town, the town will not fall. If both are unsuccessful, the military strength will be exhausted. The general will be alone and find himself cut off from his men and the soldiers will disobey the orders. If such soldiers are used to defend a position, the position can not be secured while if they are used to fight a war, they will flee. Such an army is called a slack army. In a slack army, the general will lose his awesomeness and authority. While a general loses awesomeness and authority, his men will disdain punishment; while the men disdain punishment, the army will be in chaos and disorder; while the army is in chaos and disorder, the soldiers will run off; while the soldiers run off, the enemy will take advantage of it; while the enemy takes the advantage, the army will inevitably be defeated and perish.

The Military Prophecies states: "An exemplary general, in his command of the army, governs and takes good care of his men as he would like to be treated himself. If he spreads his kind-

【原文】

人。推惠施恩，士力日新，战如风发，攻如河决。”故其众可望而不可当，可下而不可胜。以身先人，故其兵为天下雄。

《军谶》曰：“军以赏为表，以罚为里。”赏罚明，则将威行；官人得，则士卒服；所任贤，则敌国震。

《军谶》曰：“贤者所适，其前无敌。”故士可下而不可骄，将可乐而不可忧，谋可深而不可疑。

【今译】

恕己之道体贴、关怀部属。普遍施予恩惠，士兵的战斗力就会日益增强。从事作战如同暴风一样迅速猛烈，投入进攻如同河水溃决一样锐不可挡。”所以，这样的军队，能够让敌人望风披靡而不敢阻挡，只能束手投降而不敢存有取胜的奢望。将领能够身先士卒，因此他所指挥的军队就可以称雄于天下。

《军谶》上说：“军队以奖赏为表，以惩罚为里，(两者缺一不可)。”赏罚严明，将帅的威信才能树立；选拔官佐得当，士卒就会心悦诚服；所委任的人贤明通达，敌国就会震恐不安。

《军谶》上说：“贤人所治理的国家，一定是所向无敌。”所以，对士大夫要谦卑恭敬而不可骄横简慢，对将帅应令其愉快而别使他陷入于忧虑，对谋略要深思熟虑而不可迟疑不决。对士大夫骄横简慢，

ness and extends his beneficence as a rule, the capacity of his army will increase day by day. They will sweep the battlefield like a hurricane and attack the enemy like a flood breaking away from a river." Facing such an army, the enemy will flee helter-skelter and dare not withstand it, will surrender and never expect to win. When the general leads his men in battle, the army in his command will be invincible.

The Military Prophecies states: "The army takes rewards as its external form and punishments as its internal substance (both are necessary and neither can go alone)." Only with clear rewards and strict punishments can the general's awesomeness be established; and when the right officers are selected, the troops will be obedient and completely convinced and when the appointed are wise and reasonable, the enemy state will be frightened and worried.

The Military Prophecies states: "A state that has worthy people to submit to its authority will be invincible." Thus the literati should be treated respectfully but not arrogantly; the generals should be pleased but not troubled and the strategies should be made after repeated deliber-

【原文】

士骄则下不顺，将忧则内外不相信，谋疑则敌国奋。以此攻伐，则致乱。夫将者，国之命也。将能制胜，则国家安定。

《军谶》曰："将能清，能静，能平，能整，能受谏，能听讼，能纳人，能采言，能知国俗，能图山川，能表险难，能制军权。"故曰：仁贤之智，圣明之虑，负薪之言，廊庙之语，兴衰之事，将所宜闻。

【今译】

下属就不会顺服；将帅内心有隐忧，君主与将帅之间就会互不信任；谋略迟疑犹豫，敌国就会振奋鼓舞。在这种状态下从事攻伐，就会招致祸乱。将帅是国家命脉之所系，将帅能克敌制胜，国家才可以长治久安。

《军谶》上说："将领应该能清廉，能沉静，能公平，能整肃，能接受规谏，能判明是非，能揽纳人才，能博采众议，能了解各诸侯国风俗，能通晓山川形势，能明了险阻要隘，能控制军队权柄。"所以说，仁人贤士的智慧，英明的谋虑，黎民百姓的议论，朝廷上的奏议，兴衰成败的史迹，身为将领者都应该有所了解。

ation but not in hesitation. If the literati are treated arrogantly, the subordinates will not be submissive; if the generals are troubled, the emperor and the generals will distrust each other; if the strategies are made in hesitation, the enemy state will feel inspired. If an attack is launched under such conditions, chaos will result. Generals are the fate of a state. Only when they are able to defeat the enemy and win victory, can a state enjoy prolonged peace and stability.

The Military Prophecies states: "The general should be able to be incorruptible, to be placid, and to be fair; he should be able to control, able to accept criticism, able to judge right and wrong, able to attract and employ the talented, able to select and accept advice, able to be aware of the customs of each state, able to know the mountains and rivers, able to understand the defiles and able to wield military power." So it is said that the wisdom of the benevolent and the virtuous, the thoughts and considerations of the emperor, the words of the ordinary people, the discussions in court and the history of ascension and decline are all what a general should be aware of.

【原文】

将者能思士如渴，则策从焉。夫将拒谏，则英雄散；策不从，则谋士叛；善恶同，则功臣倦；专己，则下归咎；自伐，则下少功；信谗，则众离心；贪财，则奸不禁；内顾，则士卒淫。将有一，则众不服；有二，则军无式；有三，则下奔北；有四，则祸及国。

【今译】

将领能够思求贤士如饥如渴，就会对贤士的谋划从善如流。将领如果拒绝规谏，英雄豪杰就会离散；不采纳谋士的策略，谋士就会叛离；善恶混同不分，功臣就会心灰意懒；个人专断，下属就会归罪于上司；自我夸耀，部下就不会积极建功；听信谗言，部众就会离心离德；贪图钱财，奸邪就无法得到禁绝；迷恋女色，士卒就会纵欲淫乱。将领如果犯有上面的一条，那么兵众就不会信服他的权威；犯有上面的两条，那么军队就会丧失法纪乱成一团；犯有上面的三条，那么部众就会纷纷逃散溃不成军；犯有上面的四条，那么大祸就会临头，殃及国家的生存。

If the general thinks of and looks for the virtuous and wise as if to quench his thirst, their advice and plans then can be followed readily. If the general stifles advice, men of character and valor will leave him. If the plans of strategists are not followed, the strategists will rebel and run away. If good and evil are treated alike, meritorious officials will be downhearted. If the general acts peremptorily, his subordinates will shirk their responsibility and impute the blame to him. If the general brags about himself, his men will not perform meritorious service vigorously. If the general believes slander, he will lose the hearts of his troops. If the general is greedy, treachery will not be checked. If the general is preoccupied with women, his officers and men will become licentious. If the general has one of these faults, his men will lose their faith in his authority. If he is marked by two of them, the army will lack discipline and order and be thrown into confusion. If he is marked by three of them, his men will be routed and flee pell-mell. If he is marked by four, then the state itself will be put in dreadful trouble and its survival will be jeopardized.

【原文】

《军谶》曰："将谋欲密，士众欲一，攻敌欲疾。"将谋密，则奸心闭；士众一，则军心结；攻敌疾，则备不及设。军有此三者，则计不夺。将谋泄，则军无势；外窥内，则祸不制；财入营，则众奸会。将有此三者，军必败。

将无虑，则谋士去；将无勇，则吏士恐；将妄动，则军不重；将迁怒，则一军惧。《军谶》曰：

【今译】

《军谶》上说："将领的谋略应做到保密，士兵的意志应做到统一，攻击敌人应做到迅疾。"将领的谋略保密，奸细就无隙可乘；士兵的意志统一，全军上下就会同心戮力；攻击敌人迅疾，敌人就会猝不及防。军队拥有这三项条件，那么计划就不会遭到挫折。将领的谋略被泄露，军队就会丧失有利态势；敌人窥探到我方的内情，祸患就会无法制止；不义之财进入军营，各种弊端就会纷至沓来。将领若犯有这三条，那么军队就会必败无疑。

将领没有深谋远虑，有智谋的士人就会失望离去；将领没有勇武气概，官兵们就会恐惧不安；将领轻举妄动，军队就不会稳重；将领迁怒于人，全军上下就会心怀畏惧。《军谶》上说："善于谋划，

The Military Prophecies states: "The strategies of the general should be kept secret. The will of the troops should be unified. The attack should be launched swiftly." If the general's strategies are kept secret, there will leave no opportunity for spies to take. If the troops' will is unified, the whole army will unite in a concerted effort. If the attack is launched swiftly, the enemy will be taken by surprise and have no time to get prepared. If an army meets these three requirements, its plan will not fail. If the general's strategies are disclosed, the army will lose its advantages. If outside agents spy out the internal information, disasters will not be prevented from occurring. If the undeserved wealth gets into the army, corrupt practices will come in succession. If the general is marked by these three, the army will inevitably be defeated.

If the general is not resourceful and farsighted, his strategists will abandon him. If the general is not courageous and brave, his officers and men will panic and worry. If the general acts impetuously, the army will not act with discretion. If the general transfers his anger to his men, the whole army will be afraid. *The Military Prophe-*

【原文】

"虑也，勇也，将之所重；动也，怒也，将之所用。"此四者，将之明诫也。

《军谶》曰："军无财，士不来；军无赏，士不往。"

《军谶》曰："香饵之下，必有悬鱼；重赏之下，必有死夫。"故礼者，士之所归；赏者，士之所死。招其所归，示其所死，则所求者至。故礼而后悔者，士不止；赏而后悔者，士不使。礼赏不倦，则士争死。

【今译】

勇武豪迈，是将领应该具备的重要品质；该动则动，该怒则怒，是将领应该掌握的用兵之道。"这四条，是将领所要时常牢记的明诫。

《军谶》上说："军队没有资财，士众就不来归附；军队没有奖赏，士众就不勇往直前。"

《军谶》上说："在香美的鱼饵引诱之下，必定有吞钩的鱼儿；在优厚的赏赐面前，必定有不怕死的士兵。"所以，使士卒相随归附的是礼遇，使士卒拚死效命的是奖赏。用礼遇招徕士众归附，用奖赏诱使士卒效命，那么，所需要的人士就会来到。因此，起初礼遇优渥而随后又反悔的，士卒就不会留下来；起初奖赏丰厚而随后又反悔的，士卒就不会听从使唤。只有礼遇奖赏一如既往，士卒才会争相效命，慷慨赴死。

cies states: "Contemplation and courage are the essential requirements a general should meet; and when to move and act and when to show his anger is what a general should know in commanding his army." These are the four precepts that a general should clearly keep in mind.

The Military Prophecies states: "If the army lacks material resources, people will not come to join it. If the army does not have rewards, the troops will lack courage to go into battle."

The Military Prophecies states: "Fragrant bait will certainly make some fish to bite the hook and big rewards will certainly make some men not afraid to die." Thus what makes officers and soldiers submit to you is courtesy and what makes them render their service at the risk of their lives is rewards. If you summon them with courtesy and make them not afraid of losing their lives with rewards, then those whom you seek will come. But if you treat them first with courtesy and then regret it, they will not stay with you; if you first reward them and afterward regret it, they will not follow your orders. Only when you respect and reward them consistently, will they be ready to render their service to you

【原文】

《军谶》曰："兴师之国，务先隆恩；攻取之国，务先养民。以寡胜众者，恩也；以弱胜强者，民也。"故良将之养士，不易于身，故能使三军如一心，则其胜可全。

《军谶》曰："用兵之要，必先察敌情。视其仓库，度其粮食，卜其强弱，察其天地，伺其空隙。"故国无军旅之难而运粮者，虚也；民菜色者，穷也。千里馈粮，民有饥色；樵苏后爨，师不宿饱。夫运

【今译】

《军谶》上说："要兴兵打仗的国家，务必事先厚施恩惠；要攻城略地的国家，务必先让民众休养生息。能够做到以少胜多，在于厚施恩惠，能够做到以弱胜强，在于获得民众的支持。"所以，优秀的将领豢养士卒，如同爱护自己的身体一样，这样才能使全军上下团结一致，万众一心，从而夺取全面的胜利。

《军谶》上说："用兵打仗的要诀，必须首先察明敌情。弄清楚它仓库的物资储存，估算它一下粮食的多少，分析判断敌人的强弱，查明敌方的天候与地理状况，寻找出敌人暴露的可乘之机。"所以，国家没有遭受战争的苦难而运送粮食的，表明国势空虚；广大民众面黄肌瘦的，表明百姓贫困。从千里之外运送粮食，民众就会面有饥色；临时砍伐柴草做饭煮粥，军队就会经常吃不饱肚子。千里之外

at the cost of their lives.

The Military Prophecies states: "A state which is about to wage a war must first make its beneficence ample. A state which is about to take cities and seize territories must first make the people recuperate and multiply. The few can defeat the many because of beneficence; the weak can defeat the strong because of the support from the people. Thus a good general should treat his troops as if they were his body, then he is able to have his army united as one and win a complete victory.

The Military Prophecies states: "To fight a war, one must first gather information about the enemy: to know about his storage of materials, estimate his food stock, analyse his strengths and weaknesses, be aware of the weather and terrain on his part and seek the advantages that can be taken on the enemy." Thus if a state which does not suffer from the scourge of a war has to transport food, it means that the state is weak and depleted; if the people look lean and haggard, it means that they are impoverished. If food has to be transported for a thousand *li*, then people will have a hungry look; if firewood has to be col-

【原文】

粮百(千)里，无一年之食；二千里，无二年之食；三千里，无三年之食，是(谓)国虚。国虚则民贫，民贫则上下不亲。敌攻其外，民盗其内，是谓必溃。

《军谶》曰：“上行虐则下急刻。赋敛重数，刑罚无极，民相残贼，是谓亡国。”

《军谶》曰：“内贪外廉，诈誉取名，窃公为

【今译】

运粮，说明国家缺一年的粮食；二千里外运粮，说明国家缺二年的粮食；三千里外运粮，说明国家缺三年的粮食。这正是国势空虚的表现。国势空虚，民众就不免贫穷；民众贫穷，上下之间就不会亲近和睦。敌人从外面进攻，民众在内部作乱，国家就必定会崩溃。

《军谶》上说：“君主肆行暴虐，臣属必定会急苛刻薄，征敛赋税又多又重，滥施刑罚漫无止境，民众蜂起自相残害，这样，国家就必定要灭亡。”

《军谶》上说：“内心贪婪而表面上装作廉洁，骗取荣誉盗取功名，窃用公家的财产来私树恩惠，

lected before cooking, it means that the army very often does not have enough food to feed its men. If food has to be transported for a thousand *li*, it means that the state lacks one year's food; if food has to be transported for two thousand *li*, it means that the state lacks two years' food; if food has to be transported for three thousand *li*, it means that the state lacks three years' food. This indicates that the state is weak and depleted. If a state is weak and depleted, the populace will be impoverished; if the populace is impoverished, the government and the governed will be estranged. If the enemy attacks from outside and the populace causes trouble from inside, the state then is doomed to collapse.

The Military Prophecies states: "When a ruler is tyrannical and cruel, his subordinates will be harsh and relentless, the taxes will be onerous, punishments will be endless and the masses will rise to destroy each other among themselves. Such a state is doomed to perish."

The Military Prophecies states: "To appear to be incorruptible while very corruptible and greedy in actuality, to obtain honor and fame by cheating, to steal from the state to distribute their

【原文】

恩，令上下昏，饰躬正颜，以获高官，是谓盗端。”

《军谶》曰：“群吏朋党，各进所亲，招举奸枉，抑挫仁贤，背公立私，同位相讪，是谓乱源。”

《军谶》曰：“强宗聚奸，无位而尊，威无不震，葛藟相连，种德立恩，夺在位权，侵侮下民，国内哗喧，臣蔽不言，是谓乱根。”

【今译】

使得上下昏聩不识其真实的面目，装出一副道貌岸然的模样，以此猎取高官厚禄，这叫做窃国的发端。”

《军谶》上说：“大小官吏拉帮结伙，各自任用自己的亲信，招纳网罗奸邪之徒，压制贬抑仁人贤士，背弃国家谋取私利，同僚之间互相讥讽攻讦，这就是国家祸乱的本源。”

《军谶》上说：“豪门望族相聚为奸，虽无爵位却尊荣富贵，威风凛凛肆无忌惮，势力如同葛藤一般盘根错节，以小恩小惠树立营造自己的形象，窃夺执政者的权力，侵害和凌辱普通民众，国内舆论大哗，大臣却隐瞒实情而不敢如实直言，这就是发生动乱的根源。”

own beneficence, thus to confuse the superiors and subordinates to cover their true colors and to pose as a person of high morals in order to gain high position and fat salary, this is referred to as the beginning of the stealing of the power of a state."

The Military Prophecies states: "Government officials form parties and cliques, recommend persons whom they are familiar with and trust, appoint the evil and corrupt, insult and repress the benevolent and virtuous, seek personal gain against the interest of the state and disparage each other, this is termed the source of state calamity and chaos."

The Military Prophecies states: "Powerful families and great clans band together, enjoy honor and wealth though without title of nobility, behave wantonly with a majestic looking, intertwine like the vines with twisted roots and gnarled branches, establish their own image with petty favors, snatch the power belonging to those in official position and harm and insult ordinary people, while within the state, there is clamoring and backbiting and ministers conceal facts and dare not tell the truth, this is called the source of

【原文】

《军谶》曰："世世作奸，侵盗县官，进退求便，委曲弄文，以危其君，是谓国奸。"

《军谶》曰："吏多民寡，尊卑相若，强弱相虏，莫适禁御，延及君子，国受其咎。"

《军谶》曰："善善不进，恶恶不退，贤者隐蔽，不肖在位，国受其害。"

《军谶》曰："枝叶强大，比周居势，卑贱陵

【今译】

《军谶》上说："世世代代为非作歹，侵犯官府，盗窃国库，出仕或退隐只求自己的方便，舞文弄墨，矫饰诡辩，危害自己的君主，这叫做捣乱国家的奸贼。"

《军谶》上说："官多而民少，尊卑上下没有区别，以强凌弱，无从禁止，祸患延及正人君子，结果使国家蒙受其害。"

《军谶》上说："喜欢好人但不加以任用，厌恶坏人但不予以黜退，德才兼备的人归隐山林，品德不端之徒把持权力，国家就会受到危害。"

《军谶》上说："宗室势力强大显赫，结党营

turmoil."

The Military Prophecies states: "They commit misdeeds and crimes generation after generation, encroach on government officials and steal the state treasury, take a post or retire due to their own convenience, engage in phrase-mongering, affectation and sophism, thus endangering their sovereign, these people are referred to as the state's treacherous ones."

The Military Prophecies states: "When there are too many officials and too few people, when there is no distinction between the honored and the lowly, when the strong bully the weak and are not prohibited, then the curse will extend to the good people and the state will suffer as a result."

The Military Prophecies states: "Fancy good people but not employ them, hate evil people but not dismiss them, and virtuous and talented persons will retire and withdraw from society into the forests and mountains and immoral people will hold positions and have power, then the state will suffer."

The Military Prophecies states: "If the sovereign's relatives and powerful families are

【原文】

(淩)贵，久而益大，上不忍废，国受其败。”

《军谶》曰：“佞臣在上，一军皆讼，引威自与，动违于众。无进无退，苟然取容。专任自己，举措伐功。诽谤盛德，诬述庸庸。无善无恶，皆与己同。稽留行事，命令不通。造作奇政，变古易常。

【今译】

私，窃据高位，欺下犯上，时间越久，他们的权势就越大，君主不忍心果断地加以铲除，国家势必遭受败亡之祸。”

《军谶》上说：“谗佞之臣在上当权，全军上下都会不满指控。他们倚仗权势，自我吹嘘，动辄违忤大家的意愿。他们在进退问题上毫无原则，只知道依照上司的脸色行事。他们刚愎自用，一举一动都夸功自傲。他们诽谤品德高尚的人，诬蔑其为庸庸碌碌之辈。他们不分善恶是非，一切只看是否合乎自己的意愿或口味。他们积压政务，使得上令不能够顺利下达，处处标新立异，变更古制，改易常

strong and large, form cliques to pursue selfish interests, occupy high positions by foul means and insult the inferior and rebel against the superior, then with the passing of time they will grow more and more powerful and if the sovereign can not bear to dismiss them, the state will undoubtedly suffer defeat from it."

The Military Prophecies states: "If sycophantic courtiers hold superior and powerful positions, the army will be full of resentments and complaints. They rely on their power to brag about themselves and rarely pay attention to the will of the masses. Their taking office or retiring are based on nothing but the likes and dislikes of their superiors. They are self-willed and leave no means untried to claim credit and sing their own praise. They slander those of great virtue and underrate them as mediocre and incompetent persons. They do not love the good nor shun the evil; whatever they do is done in accordance with their own will and taste. They do not conduct administrative affairs so that commands and orders are not followed readily. They always do something unconventional and unorthodox, altering ancient traditions and changing common

【原文】

君用佞人，必受祸殃。”

《军谶》曰：“奸雄相称，障蔽主明；毁誉并兴，壅塞主聪。各阿所以(私)，令主失忠。”

故主察异言，乃睹其萌；主聘儒贤，奸雄乃遁；主任旧齿，万事乃理；主聘岩穴，士乃得实。谋及负薪，功乃可述；不失人心，德乃洋溢。

【今译】

法。君主若是重用这样的奸佞之徒，必定会受到他们的祸害。”

《军谶》上说：“奸雄之间相互称许，遮蔽君主的视线，使得其是非不分；毁谤和吹嘘搅和在一起，堵塞君主的听觉，使得其善恶难辨。他们各自偏袒自己的私党同伙，使得君主失去忠义之臣。”

因此，君主洞察诡异的言辞，才能看出祸乱的萌芽。君主礼聘儒士贤才，奸雄宵小就会落荒逃遁。君主任用年高德劭的老臣，所有事情就会处理得井井有条。君主征聘那些山林隐士，才能得到有真才实学的治国之才。君主在运筹划策之时若能倾听黎民百姓的意见，他的功业就可以书诸竹帛，永垂青史。君主如果能够做到不失民心，他的盛名美德就可以远播四方，广为传颂。

practices. If the sovereign employs such wanton characters, he will no doubt suffer from them."

The Military Prophecies states: "Evil men praise each other so as to blindfold the sovereign and make him unable to distinguish between right and wrong. They blend slanders with flatters so as to obfuscate the sovereign's wisdom and make him unable to tell good from evil. They favor members of their own clique so as to make the sovereign lose loyal court officials."

Accordingly, if the sovereign has discerning eyes for absurd remarks, then he will discover the omen of chaos. If the sovereign engages scholars and virtuous talents with courtesy, evil men will flee. If the sovereign employs worthy men of experience and age, all affairs will be well managed. If the sovereign invites those worthies who have withdrawn into the mountains, he will get those who are real capable of running the state. If the sovereign can listen to the opinions of the ordinary people, his achievements might be written down and have a niche in history. If the sovereign does not lose the hearts of the people, his name and virtue will be widely spread and eulogized everywhere.

卷中

中略

【原文】

夫三皇无言而化流四海，故天下无所归功。帝者，体天则地，有言有令，而天下太平。君臣让功，四海化行，百姓不知其所以然。故使臣不待礼赏有功，美而无害。王者，制人以道，降心服志，设矩备衰，四海会同，王职不废，虽有甲兵之备，而无

【今译】

三皇默默无言，但他们的教化却流布于四海，所以天下的人不知道应该把功劳归属给哪个人。五帝顺应天地间的自然规律，设教施令，天下因此而太平无事。君臣互相推让功名，四海之内教化大行，黎民百姓却不知其中的缘由。所以，役使臣僚而不必依靠礼法赏赐其功劳，就能够使君臣之间和美无间。三王运用道德统御民众，使他们心悦诚服，制定各种法规以预防衰败，天下诸侯定时前来朝觐天子，向朝廷奉献贡赋。虽然拥有军备，但没有战争的祸患。君主对臣僚深信无猜忌，臣僚对君主也没有疑心，国家稳定，君主平安，臣属下僚依据义的规范适时告退，君臣之间也能够和睦美满而不互相

BOOK II

MIDDLE STRATEGY

The Three Kings never said anything, but the moralization had been felt all over the world, and the people did not know to whom to attribute the accomplishments. The Five Emperors formulated and gave instructions and orders in accordance with the law of nature and the world therefore attained great peace. The sovereign and the ministers yielded the credit to each other, while the world was well moralized with the ordinary people not conscious of how all this had come about. Thus the sovereign needed not rely on the forms of propriety and rewards in employing his subordinates, and there was peace and harmony between him and his subordinates. The Three Kings ruled by benevolence, causing the people to be completely convinced and submit willingly while also establishing various

【原文】

斗战之患。君无疑于臣，臣无疑于主，国定主安，臣以义退，亦能美而无害。霸者，制士以权，结士以信，使士以赏。信衰则士疏，赏亏则士不用命。

《军势》曰：“出军行师，将在自专。进退内御，则功难成。”

《军势》曰：“使智，使勇，使贪，使愚。”智者乐立其功，勇者好行其志，贪者邀趋其利，愚者不

【今译】

伤害。五霸利用权术来驾御士人，依靠信用来结交士人，借助奖赏来役使士人。信任差了士人就会对他疏远，奖赏少了士人就会不肯用力效命。

《军势》上说：“出兵打仗，贵在将帅拥有机断行事的权限。如果进退行动都受到君主的掣肘牵制，那么就难以取得成功。”

《军势》上说：“使用有智谋的人，使用勇敢的人，使用贪婪的人，使用愚笨的人，（其方法各有不同）。”有智谋的人乐于建功立业，勇敢的人喜欢实现自己的志向，贪婪的人热衷于追求利禄，愚笨

laws and regulations against decline. All the feudal lords throughout the country came to a regular audience with the emperor and presented tribute to the court. Although they made military preparations, they never suffered from the scourge of war. The sovereign did not doubt his subordinates, while the subordinates had faith in their sovereign. The state was settled, the sovereign was secured and the bureaucrats resigned with righteousness at an appropriate time, so the sovereign and his subordinates could be able to coexist in harmony without harm. The Five Hegemons controlled their officials by political trickery, treated them with trust and used them with rewards. When the trust declined, the officials would become estranged; when rewards became inadequate, they would not try their best to render their service.

The Military Power states: "To fight a war, generals must have their own authority to exercise power. If the advancing and withdrawing are all controlled by the emperor, it will be hard to attain success."

The Military Power states: "Employ the wise, the courageous, the greedy and the stupid (in a

【原文】

顾其死。因其至情而用之，此军之微权也。

《军势》曰：“无使辩士谈说敌美，为其惑众；无使仁者主财，为其多施而附于下。”

《军势》曰：“禁巫祝，不得为吏士卜问军之吉凶。”

《军势》曰：“使义士不以财。”故义者不为不仁者死，智者不为暗主谋。

【今译】

的人从来不顾惜自己的性命。根据他们的特殊个性加以充分利用，这是治军用人方面莫测高深的权术。

《军势》上说：“不要让能言善辩的家伙谈论敌人的长处，因为这会蛊惑众人；也不要让心地仁慈的人主管财物，因为他会滥施赏财物以讨好迎合下属。”

《军势》上说：“在军队之中要禁绝巫祝，决不准他们为官兵占卜军队的吉凶祸福。”

《军势》上说：“任使侠义之士不必依靠财物。”因为侠义之士不会为那些不仁不义之辈去效死，而足智多谋之士也不会为昏聩的君主去出谋划策。

way to their respective characteristics)." The wise take pleasure in establishing credits and achievements. The courageous like to realize their ambitions. The greedy fervently pursue wealth and position. The stupid do not care very much for their lives. Make the best use of them in accordance with their respective characteristics, for this is the profound art to run an army and to employ men."

The Military Power states. "Do not allow those who are eloquent to discuss the enemy's merits because they may confuse the masses. Do not let those who are benevolent to control the finances because they may dispense too much in order to please their subordinates."

The Military Power states: "Prohibit sorcerers from the army and do not allow them to divine about the army's good or evil and fortune or misfortune on behalf of the officers and soldiers."

The Military Power states: "One does not have to depend on material wealth to employ noble-minded men." For the noble-minded will not die for the malevolent and the wise will not give advice to and make plans for an obtuse ruler.

【原文】

主不可以无德，无德则臣叛；不可以无威，无威则失权。臣不可以无德，无德则无以事君；不可以无威，无威则国弱，威多则身蹶。

故圣王御世，观盛衰，度得失，而为之制。故诸侯二师，方伯三师，天子六师。世乱则叛逆生，王泽竭，则盟誓相诛伐。德同势敌，无以相倾，乃揽英雄之心，与众同好恶，然后加之以权变。故非

【今译】

君主不能没有道德，没有道德臣属就会背叛；不可以没有威仪，没有威仪就会丧失权力。臣僚们不能没有道德，没有道德就无法侍奉和辅佐君主；不可以没有威势，没有威势国家就会遭到削弱。但是，如果威势过于膨胀，也会使自己身败名裂。

因此，圣王统御治理天下，观察世道的盛衰，推究政治的得失，从而制定出典章礼乐制度。规定诸侯拥有二个师的兵力，方伯拥有三个师的兵力，天子拥有六个师的兵力。后世社会动乱，叛逆随之发生，天子的恩泽也同样趋于枯竭，结果是导致诸侯之间结盟立誓，互相征伐。他们之间道德上优劣相同，实力上强弱相当，谁也无法战胜对方。于是就收揽英雄豪杰之心，与大家同好共恶，然后再加

A sovereign can not be without virtue, for if he lacks virtue, his subordinates will betray him; he can neither be without awesomeness, for if he lacks awesomeness, he will lose his power. A minister can not be without virtue, for if he lacks virtue he will not be able to serve and assist the sovereign; he can neither be without awesomeness, for if he lacks awesomeness, the state will be weakened. However, too much awesomeness can also bring disgrace and ruin upon himself.

Therefore the Sage Kings, in governing the country, observed the flourishing and decline of the society, studied the gains and losses of the policies and created laws and institutions. Thus it was stipulated that the feudal lords have two armies, the regional earls have three armies and the Son of Heaven has six. Later, the country was turbulent and rebellions were born, and the Son of Heaven's bountiful influence was to be exhausted. As a result, the feudal lords entered into alliance and swore oaths and started to attack each other. They were matched with each other either in virtue or in strength and no one could defeat the other. Then you must win the heart of the valiant, share likes and dislikes with

【原文】

计策无以决嫌定疑，非谲奇无以破奸息寇，非阴谋无以成功。

圣人体天，贤者法地，智者师古。是故《三略》为衰世作。《上略》设礼赏，别奸雄，著成败。《中略》差德行，审权变。《下略》陈道德，察安危，明贼贤之咎。故人主深晓《上略》，则能任贤擒敌；深晓《中略》，则能御将统众；深晓《下略》，

【今译】

之使用权术，随机应变。所以，不经过运筹策划，就没有办法来裁决疑惑难明的事情；不采取诡诈奇谲的手段，就没有办法来打击奸人消灭敌寇；不施用阴谋诡计，也就没有办法取得成功。

圣人能够体察上天之道，贤人能够取法大地之理，睿智多谋者能够以历史为鉴。因此，《三略》一书是专门为衰乱的时代而写作的。其中《上略》部分主要讲述设置礼赏，辨识奸雄，昭示成功或失败的根源等方面的道理。《中略》部分主要阐述区分德行，审达权变等方面的精髓要义。《下略》部分则主要是阐述道德，体察安危，揭示迫害贤人的罪过和后果。因此，身为君主的深通《上略》，就能够任用贤人，制服敌人；深通《中略》，就能够驾御将帅，统辖士众；深通《下略》，就能够明察天下盛

the common people, and resort to the art of trickery and change according to circumstances. Thus without stratagems, you will not be able to justify suspicions and settle doubts; without treacherous and strange means, you will not be able to crack down on evildoers and wipe out the enemy; and without schemes and intrigues, you will not be successful.

The Sages can observe and understand the way of how to act in Heaven, the virtuous can be aware of the laws of how to act on Earth and the wise can learn lessons from history. Therefore, the *Three Strategies* has been written for a period of decline and turbulence. The "Superior Strategy" tells about the establishment of the forms of propriety and rewards, the discrimination between evildoers and the valiant and reasons of success and defeat. The "Middle Strategy" gives an account of the moral conduct and changes of power. The "Inferior Strategy" explicates morality and virtue, security and danger and displays the wrongs and results of persecuting virtuous people. Thus if the ruler thoroughly understands the "Superior Strategy", he will be able to employ the virtuous and conquer the enemy; if he thoroughly understands the "Middle

【原文】

则能明盛衰之源，审治国之纪。人臣深晓《中略》，则能全功保身。

夫高鸟死，良弓藏；敌国灭，谋臣亡。亡者，非丧其身也，谓夺其威，废其权也。封之于朝，极人臣之位，以显其功；中州善国，以富其家；美色珍玩，以说(悦)其心。

夫人众一合而不可卒离，威权一与而不可卒移。

【今译】

衰兴亡的缘由，了解和掌握治理国家的一般原则。身为臣子的深通《中略》，就能够成就功业，保全性命。

高翔的鸟儿死光了，优良的弓箭就会被收藏起来；敌对的国家灭亡了，谋臣就会被加以消灭。所谓“消灭”，并不是指消灭他的肉体，而是指削夺他的威势，废除他的权力。在朝廷上对他进行封赏，给他群臣中最尊贵的爵位，以此来表彰他的功劳；赐封给他中原地区最丰沃的土地，使得他家业殷富；赏赐给他珍玩和美女，使得他心情快乐。

民众一经组合为军队，便不宜仓促解散；权力一旦授予，便不可仓促变动。战事结束、将帅班师

Strategy" , he will be able to control the generals and command the troops; if he thoroughly understands the "Inferior Strategy", he will be able to discern the reason of flourishing and decline and understand and master the way and general principles to govern a state. As for his subordinates, if they thoroughly understand the "Middle Strategy", they will be able to achieve merit and preserve their lives.

When the soaring birds have all been slain, the good bows are stored away. When enemy states have been extinguished, resourceful court officials are destroyed. Here "destroy" does not mean that they have been destroyed physically but that their awesomeness has been taken away and power removed. They will be enfeoffed in court, being given the highest ranks of nobility among other officials as to manifest their merits and achievements. They will be presented with the richest lands in the Central Plains in order to enrich their families. They will be bestowed with rare curios and beautiful women in order to make them happy.

Now once the masses are brought together and form an army, they should not be dismissed

【原文】

还师罢军，存亡之阶。故弱之以位，夺之以国，是谓霸者之略。故霸者之作，其论驳也。存社稷、罗英雄者，《中略》之势也。故世主秘焉。

【今译】

回朝，这是君主权位存亡的关键时刻。所以，要通过赐封爵位的办法来削弱将帅的实力，通过赐予土地的办法来剥夺将帅的权柄，这就是称雄为霸者驾御将帅的高明方略。因此说，称雄为霸者的所作所为，其道理是十分驳杂的。保全国家，网罗英雄，就是《中略》所阐述的权变诀窍。对此，历代君主都匠心独运，秘而不宣。

hastily. Once authority is granted, it should not be shifted suddenly. When the war ends and the generals return, it is a time critical for the ruler to preserve or lose his position and power. Thus he should weaken the generals by means of presenting them with titles of nobility and remove their commanding power by means of giving them lands and this is a wise strategy for one to become a hegemon and to control the generals. So, how to act for a ruler to become a hegemon is very complicated. To preserve the state and gather those of character and courage is the secret of the "Middle Strategy" about the shift of power, on which all previous monarchs had exercised their own minds and always kept their thoughts a secret.

卷下

下略

【原文】

夫能扶天下之危者，则据天下之安；能除天下之忧者，则享天下之乐；能救天下之祸者，则获天下之福。故泽及于民，则贤人归之；泽及昆虫，则圣人归之。贤人所归，则其国强；圣人所归，则六

【今译】

能够匡扶天下于危亡之际的人，就能拥有天下的安宁；能够祛除天下于忧患之中的人，就能享有天下的快乐；能够拯救天下于灾难深渊的人，就能获得天下的福祉。所以，能遍施恩泽于广大民众，贤人就会归附他；能遍施恩泽于昆虫万物，圣人就会归附他。贤人一旦前来归附，那么这个国家就会强盛；圣人一旦前来归附，那么就可以一统天下。要依靠行德来罗致贤人，凭借履道来招徕圣人。贤

BOOK III

INFERIOR STRATEGY

Now one who can help all those in peril under Heaven will enjoy peace under Heaven. One who can remove the distress of all those under Heaven will enjoy pleasure under Heaven. One who can rescue all those under Heaven suffering from misfortune will enjoy happiness under Heaven. Therefore, when the ruler's bounties extend to the great masses, virtuous men will come to give him their allegiance. When his bounties extend to insects and all creatures, sages will come to give him their allegiance. When virtuous people give him their allegiance, his state will be strong; when sages give him their allegiance, all countries under Heaven will be unified and put under his command. One recruits virtuous men through virtue and attracts sages through doctrines. If the

【原文】

合同。求贤以德，致圣以道。贤去，则国微；圣去，则国乖。微者，危之阶；乖者，亡之徵。

贤人之政，降人以体；圣人之政，降人以心。体降可以图始，心降可以保终。降体以礼，降心以乐。所谓乐者，非金石丝竹也，谓人乐其家，谓人乐其族，谓人乐其业，谓人乐其都邑，谓人乐其政

【今译】

人离去，国家就会衰微；圣人离去，国家就会混乱。国家衰微，是走向危险的途径；国家混乱，是陷于灭亡的征兆。

贤人的政治，是使人们在行动上做到顺从；圣人的政治，是使人们从内心深处真诚依顺。使人们行动顺从，可以谋划开创事业；使人们内心顺从，可以确保善始善终。使人们行动顺从依靠的是礼，使人们内心顺从依靠的是乐。所谓“乐”，并非是指金、石、丝、竹这一类乐器，而是指人们喜爱他们的家庭，是指人们喜爱他们的宗族，是指人们喜爱他们的职业，是指人们喜爱他们所居住的城邑，是指人们拥护国家的政令，是指人们乐于讲究道德。这样治理国家的君主，就能推行乐教来陶冶和节制人们的行为，使人们不丧失和谐的关系。所以，有

virtuous men depart, the state will become weak. If the sages leave, the state will be in disorder. Weakness will lead a state to peril and disorder is a sign of doom.

The government of a virtuous man causes people to submit with their bodies. Thegovem-ment of a sage causes people to submit with their minds. When people submit with their bodies, you can plan to begin your course; when people submit with their minds,your course will not only begin well but also end well. Physical submission will be attained through ruling with propriety, while mental submission will be attained through "music." What is referred to here as "music" is not the sound of such musical instruments as made of metal,stone, string and bamboo. What "music" refers to here is the pleasure people take in their families, clans, occupations and their towns and cities and is that people support their government, the ethics and moralities. To rule a state in this fashion, the ruler will be able to use such "music" to influence and control the activities of his people and create a harmonious relationship.

【原文】

令，谓人乐其道德。如此君人者，乃作乐以节之，使不失其和。故有德之君，以乐乐人；无德之君，以乐乐身。乐人者，久而长；乐身者，不久而亡。

释近谋远者，劳而无功；释远谋近者，佚而有终。佚政多忠臣，劳政多怨民。故曰：务广地者荒，务广德者强。能有其有者安，贪人之有者残。残灭之政，累世受患。造作过制，虽成必败。

舍己而教人者逆，正己而化人者顺。逆者乱之

【今译】

道德的君主，总是用乐来使人们快乐；无道德的君主，总是用乐来使自己快乐。使人们快乐的，国家长治久安；光使自己快乐的，国家不久就会灭亡。

舍近而图远的人，必定劳而无功；舍远而图近的人，必定安逸而善终。安逸的政治，就会出现众多忠臣；烦苛的政治，就会产生许多怨民。所以说，追求向外扩张领土的，内政必然会荒废；致力于广施恩德的，国势必然会强盛。能保有自己所当拥有的，就平安无事；贪图他人所有的，就受辱招损。残酷暴虐的政治，世世代代都会遭受祸患。所作所为超越了常规，即便暂时取得成功，但最终仍将归于失败。

撇开自己而去教训别人这属于违背常理，首先端正自身再去教化别人这才合乎常理。违背常理乃

Thus a virtuous ruler uses " music" to give pleasure to his people, while a debauched ruler uses "music" to pleasure himself. If a ruler gives pleasure to his people, his state will be in good order and peace for long; if a ruler only pleasures himself, the state will soon perish.

If one abandons what lies close at hand for what is afar, his work will come to no avail; if one abandons what is afar for what lies nearby, he will be at ease and come to a good end. To govern with ease, there will be many loyal ministers; to govern with cruelty, there will be a lot of resentful people. Thus it is said: "If one seeks to broaden his territory, public duties and state affairs will be neglected. If one concentrates on broadening his virtues and bounties, the state will grow strong and prosperous." One who is able to hold what he should possess will be safe; one who is greedy for what others have will be disgraced and destroyed. A cruel and tyrannical government will entangle later generations in misfortune. If one acts against common practice, he might be successful for a period of time, but will be defeated ultimately.

Indulging oneself while lecturing others is

【原文】

招，顺者治之要。

道、德、仁、义、礼，五者一体也。道者，人之所蹈；德者，人之所得；仁者，人之所亲；义者，人之所宜；礼者，人之所体。不可无一焉。故夙兴夜寐，礼之制也；讨贼报仇，义之决也；恻隐之心，仁之发也；得己得人，德之路也；使人均平，不失其所，道之化也。

出君下臣名曰命，施于竹帛名曰令，奉而行之

【今译】

是招致祸乱的根源，合乎常理才是安定国家的关键。

道、德、仁、义、礼，这五者是一个完整的体系。道是人们所应该遵循的法则，德是人们所应该持有的情操，仁是人们所应该保持的亲情，义是人们所应该去做的合宜事情，礼是人们所应该身体力行的规范。这五者缺一不可。所以，人们早起而晚睡，这是受礼的约束；讨伐贼寇报仇雪恨，这是出于义的决断；同情怜悯之心，这乃是发自于仁慈的本性；使自己和他人都获得满足，这是行施德的要求；使人均齐平等，各得其所，这是推广道的教化。

由君主下达给臣下的指示叫做“命”，把它书写在竹帛上叫做“令”，遵照和执行命令叫做“政”。

abnormal. Rectifying yourself before lecturing others is normal. Abnormality is the source of chaos and disasters. Normality is the key to the stability of a state.

Doctrine, virtue, benevolence, righteousness and ethics are an integrated system of five in one. Doctrine refers to the laws and regulations that people should observe and follow; virtue refers to the noble sentiment that people should have; benevolence refers to the emotional attachment that people should sustain;righteousness refers to the right things that people should do; and ethics refers to the norms that people should behave themselves in accordance with. No one of these five can be neglected and lacked. Thus to get up early in the morning and go to bed late at night is restrained by ethics; to punish brigands and take revenge is decided and justified by righteousness; to have sympathy is based on one's kind nature; to try to satisfy not only oneself but also others is a requirement of virtue; to treat people equal and let them have what they should have is education and dissemination of doctrines.

The instructions given by the ruler to his

【原文】

名曰政。夫命失，则令不行；令不行，则政不正；政不正，则道不通；道不通，则邪臣胜；邪臣胜，则主威伤。

千里迎贤，其路远；致不肖，其路近。是以明王舍近而取远，故能全功，尚人，而下尽力。

废一善，则众善衰；赏一恶，则众恶归。善者

【今译】

“命”如果有差错，“令”就无法推行；“令”如果不能推行，“政”就会发生偏差；政治如有偏差，治国之“道”就会行不通；治国之“道”倘若行不通，那么奸佞之臣就会占据上风；奸佞之臣假若得势，那么君主的威权势必会受到损伤。

千里之外去迎聘贤人，路途十分遥远；但招引奸邪之徒，路途却非常近便。所以，英明的君王宁愿舍近而求远，因而能保全功业。尊尚贤人，属下便会竭尽全力加以报答。

废弃闲置一个好人，那么众多好人都会悲观丧气；奖励赏赐一个坏人，那么其他坏人就会纷至沓

subordinates are termed "commands." When they are recorded on bamboo strips and silk rolls, they are termed "orders." When people follow and implement these commands and orders, it is termed "government." When "commands" are wrong, "orders" then can not be implemented. If "orders" fail to be implemented, "government" can not be correctly established. If "government" is not correctly established, the "doctrines" to govern the state can not be followed. If "doctrines" are not followed, crafty and treacherous court officials will hold sway; if the crafty and treacherous officials are in power, the ruler's awesomeness and authority will be harmed and damaged.

To meet and invite a virtuous person a thousand *li* away, one has to cover a great distance; but to bring in crafty and evil men, it is just handy and easy. For this reason, a wise ruler prefers to abandon what is nearby for what is afar so that he will be able to preserve his merits and achievements. When virtuous people are respected and honored, subordinates will do their best in return.

If you leave one good man unused, then a lot

【原文】

得其佑，恶者受其诛，则国安而众善至。

众疑无定国，众惑无治民。疑定惑还，国乃可安。

一令逆则百令失，一恶施则百恶结。故善施于顺民，恶加于凶民，则令行而无怨。使怨治怨，是谓逆天；使仇治仇，其祸不救。治民使平，致平以

【今译】

来。好人好事得到保护，坏人坏事受到惩治，国家就会安定，而大量的好人好事便会纷纷涌现。

民众都心存疑虑，那么就不会有政治安定的国家；民众都困惑不解，那么就不会有奉公守法的百姓。只有祛除疑虑，澄清迷惑，国家才会趋于安宁。

一项政令背天逆理，其他政令也会难以收效；一桩坏事得到推行，其他坏事就会随之汇集。所以，善政施加于驯服听话的民众，酷政施加于凶恶暴戾之徒，那么政令便能顺利推行，民众也不会有什么怨言。用民众所怨恨的办法去治理怀有怨恨情绪的民众，这叫做背天逆理；用民众所仇恨的办法去治理怀有仇恨心理的民众，所招致的灾祸将无法挽救。治理民众要做到公平，而要实现公平，政治就必须清明。这样，民众就能各得其所而天下也将太平安

of good men will become disheartened; if you reward one evil man, then many evil men will keep pouring in. If the good get protected and the evil are punished, the state will be in good order and peace, and good people and good deeds will come to the fore in large numbers.

When the masses are doubtful, there will be no well-governed state. When the masses are confused, there will be no law-abiding populace. Only when doubts are settled and confusion is cleared up, can a state be secure.

If one order is given against the heavenly justice, then all other orders will not be put into effect. When one evil act is advocated, all other evils will come to the fore. Thus if you govern compliant people with benevolent policies and govern wicked people with oppressive policies, orders then can be obeyed without any discontent. To govern the discontented in a discontented way is termed "against the heavenly justice"; to govern vengeful people in a vengeful way, an irreversible disaster will result. People should be governed with justice and justice can only be done when the government is good. Then, the people will have whatever they should have and

【原文】

清，则民得其所而天下宁。

犯上者尊，贪鄙者富，虽有圣王，不能致其治；犯上者诛，贪鄙者拘，则化行而众恶消。清白之士，不可以爵禄得；节义之士，不可以威刑胁。故明君求贤，必观其所以而致焉。致清白之士，修其礼；致节义之士，修其道。而后士可致，而名可保。

夫圣人君子，明盛衰之源，通成败之端，审治乱之机，知去就之节。虽穷不处亡国之位，虽贫不

【今译】

宁。

犯上作乱的人显赫尊贵，贪婪卑鄙的人发财致富，即使有圣明的君主，也不能把国家治理好。犯上作乱的人受到诛戮，贪婪卑鄙的人受到拘禁，这样，教化才可以得到推行，邪恶的人和事情才会销声匿迹。品行高洁的人，不可以用爵禄来加以收买；讲究节操道义的人，不可以用威刑来加以胁迫。所以，英明的君主征求贤人，一定要根据他们的志向气节而加以罗致。罗致品行高洁的人，要讲究礼法；罗致有节操道义的人，要讲究道义。然后，贤士才可以被罗致到手，而君主的英名也能够得到保全。

圣人君子能明察盛衰兴亡的根源，通晓成败得失的先兆，洞悉治乱安危的关键，了解进退去就的时机。虽然仕途困穷也不做行将灭亡之国的官吏，虽然生活贫寒也不领取混乱衰败之邦的俸禄。隐名埋姓，胸怀经邦治国之道的人士，时机成熟才会有

the world will be in peace and tranquility.

If those who oppose the ruler are honored and hold high positions, while the greedy and contemptible are enriched, then even with a sage ruler, the state can not be very well governed. If those who oppose the ruler are punished and executed and the greedy and contemptible put into custody, then good social ethics will prevail and various evils will be eliminated. Noble men should not be enticed with ranks and salaries; righteous men should not be intimidated with punishment. Thus when a wise ruler seeks to attract virtuous people, he must attract them in accordance with their aspiration and interest. To attract noble men, he must observe the forms of propriety; to attract righteous men, he must value morality and justice. Only in this way can the virtuous be recruited and the ruler's reputation preserved.

Sages and virtuous men can perceive the sources of flourishing and decline, understand signs of success and defeat, have a true knowledge of the key to the management of turbulence and danger and know clearly when to take office and when to retire. Such men will not hold a

【原文】

食乱邦之禄。潜名抱道者，时至而动，则极人臣之位；德合于己，则建殊绝之功：故其道高而名扬于后世。

圣王之用兵，非乐之也，将以诛暴讨乱也。夫以义诛不义，若决江河而溉爝火，临不测而挤欲堕，其克必矣。所以优游恬淡而不进者，重伤人物也。夫兵者，不祥之器，天道恶之，不得已而用之，是

【今译】

所行动，因而能够位极人臣；遇到志向和德行与自己吻合的君主，便能建立殊世的功勋：所以，他的道术卓绝高明而名扬后世。

圣明的君主兴兵打仗，并不是出于对战争的爱好，而是将要运用战争来诛伐残暴，讨平叛乱。以正义战争诛讨非正义的战争，就好比是决开江河之水去浇灭微弱的火光，身临无底深渊去推挤一个摇摇欲坠的人，他赢得胜利乃是必然的。圣王之所以优闲恬静而不急于进击，乃是因为他不愿意过多地损伤生命和财物。用兵打仗，这是不吉祥的事物，连天道也厌恶它。只有在万不得已的情况下动用战争这一手段，这才是顺乎天道的。人们处于天道的

position in a perishing state however frustrated their official career is, and will not accept salaries from a turbulent and declining country however poor a life they live. Those who live incognito but have true knowledge of the way to govern and run a state will not take action until the right time comes, so they can reach the pinnacle which a subject can attain. When they encounter a ruler whose aspiration and virtue accord with theirs, they will be able to establish extraordinary achievements and feats. So their ways of life are brilliant and lofty and their names will be praised in later generations.

A sage king wages a war not because he loves war but because he wants to employ war against cruelty and savagery and punish the rebellious. To wage a war of justice against a war of injustice is just like releasing a river to douse a small torch, or like pushing a person tottering at the edge of an abyss. His victory is inevitable. A sage king is at ease and not in a hurry to advance and attack because he does not want to have too many living creatures injured and too many properties damaged. War is never an auspicious thing and is even abhorred by the Ethics

【原文】

天道也。夫人之在道，(若)若鱼之在水，得水而生，失水而死。故君子者常畏惧而不敢失道。

豪杰秉职，国威乃弱；杀生在豪杰，国势乃竭；豪杰低首，国乃可久；杀生在君，国乃可安。四民用灵(虚)，国乃无储；四民用足，国乃安乐。

贤臣内，则邪臣外；邪臣内，则贤臣毙。内外

【今译】

衍化之中，就如同鱼儿生活在水中，遇到水而生，离开水而死。所以，君子要时时心存敬畏而不敢须臾背离天道。

豪强把持朝廷政治，国家的威望就会被削弱；生杀大权操纵在豪强的手中，国家的势力就会趋于衰竭。豪强俯首听命，国家才可以长治久安；生杀大权由国君掌握，国家才可以保持安宁。士农工商日用匮乏，国家就没有储备；士农工商日用富足，国家方可以安乐。

贤臣在朝廷之中被亲近，奸臣就会被疏远在外；奸臣在朝廷之中被亲近，贤臣就会被置于死地。亲

of Heaven. Only when war is employed as a last resort, will it accord with the Ethics of Heaven. Men live in the evolvement of the Ethics of Heaven just like fish living in water. In water, they will live, and out of water, they will die. So, a good man must constantly have respect and fear of the Ethics of Heaven and must not run against it even for one minute.

If despots and bullies hold power in court government, the prestige of the state will be reduced; if the power of life and death lies with despots and bullies, the state strength will be weakened. If despots and bullies bow their heads in submission, the state will be secure and in good order for long. When the power of life and death lies with the sovereign, the state then will have its peace. When scholars, peasants, workers and merchants have little for their daily use, the state will run short of stores; only when scholars, peasants, workers and merchants have enough for their daily use, will the state be secure and happy.

When worthy ministers are favored inside the court, treacherous ones will get estranged and be kept outside the court; when the treacherous are

【原文】

失宜，祸乱传世。

大臣疑主，众奸集聚。臣当君尊，上下乃昏；君当臣处，上下失序。

伤贤者，殃及三世；蔽贤者，身受其害；嫉贤者，其名不全；进贤者，福流子孙。故君子急于进贤而美名彰焉。利一害百，民去城郭；利一害万，

【今译】

疏颠倒，内外失宜，祸乱就会流传给后代。

权臣自比君主，群奸就会借机聚集。臣属相当于君主那样尊崇，上下秩序便昏昧不明；君主相当于臣属的地位，上下秩序就彻底颠倒。

伤害贤人的，祸殃就会延及子孙三代；埋没贤人的，自身也会受到损害；嫉妒贤人的，个人名声便不能保全；举荐贤人的，福祉将流及子孙后代。所以，君子热心于举荐贤人而使美名显扬于世间。使一个人获利而使一百人遭受祸害，那么民众就会离开城郭；使一个人得利而使一万人遭受祸害，那

favored inside the court, the worthy will be destroyed. When being favored and being estranged are reversed and inside and outside lose what is appropriate, disaster and disorder will last through generations.

If senior court officials regard themselves as the sovereign, then a myriad of evil men will take the advantage to get together. If subordinates usurp respect that should be due the sovereign, then the relations between the upper and lower ranks will be confused. If the sovereign is put in a position of a subject, the relations between the upper and lower will be totally reversed.

If someone harms virtuous people, calamity will extend three generations. If someone stifles virtuous people, he himself will suffer the harm. If someone is jealous of virtuous people, his reputation will not be preserved. If someone recommends virtuous men, blessings will pass to his sons and grandsons. Thus if a good man is anxious to recommend the virtuous, his name will be well known by the world. If you profit one and harm a hundred, people will leave the city. If you profit one and harm ten thousand, the

【原文】

国乃思散。去一利百，人乃慕泽；去一利万，政乃不乱。

【今译】

么全国上下就会人心思散。除掉一个人而让一百人得利，那么人们就会思慕他的恩泽；除掉一个人而让一万人得利，那么政治就不会发生动乱。

populace of the state will think about dispersing. If you get rid of one and thereby profit a hundred, people will long for your bounties. If you get rid of one and thereby profit ten thousand, your government will not be disordered.

唐太宗李卫公问对
QUESTIONS AND REPLIES BETWEEN TANG TAIZONG AND LI WEIGONG

卷上

【原文】

太宗曰："高丽数侵新罗，朕遣使谕，不奉诏，将讨之，如何？"

靖曰："探知盖苏文自恃知兵，谓中国无能讨，故违命。臣请师三万擒之。"

太宗曰："兵少地遥，以何术临之？"

靖曰："臣以正兵。"

太宗曰："平突厥时用奇兵，今言正兵，何

【今译】

唐太宗说："高丽数次侵犯新罗，朕派遣使官晓谕其息兵，高丽不接受诏令，朕将兴兵讨伐它。你看此事怎样？"

李靖说："据侦察，盖苏文依仗自己懂得一些战阵之事，认为我中原王朝没能力讨伐，所以敢于违抗诏命。臣请求率三万兵马擒拿盖苏文。"

太宗说："兵少路远，你用什么办法来对付他？"

李靖说："臣用正规战法与之作战。"

太宗说："你平定突厥时用的是出敌不意的战

BOOK I

Tang Taizong (Emperor Tai Zong of the Tang Dynasty) asked: "Gaoli (Koguryo) has invaded Xinluo (Silla) several times, I dispatched an emissary to order it to stop, but Gaoli disobeyed the edict. I am about to send forth a punitive expedition on it. How do you think about it?"

Li Jing replied: "According to what we have found out, Gai Suwen, relying on the knowledge about military strategy and tactics, believes that our Central Imperial State lacks the capacity to send a punitive expedition on him. That is why he dared to disobey the edict. I request an army of thirty thousand men to capture him."

Tang Taizong said: "With so few troops and so long a distance, what tactics will you apply to fight with him?"

Li Jing said: "I will fight with him with orthodox tactics."

Tang Taizong said: "When you pacified Turk

【原文】

也?”

靖曰：“诸葛亮七擒孟获，无他道也，正兵而已矣。”

太宗曰：“晋马隆计(讨)凉州，亦是依八阵图，作偏箱车。地广，则用鹿角车营；路狭，则为木屋施于车上，且战且前。信乎，正兵古人所重也!”

靖曰：“臣讨突厥，西行数千里。若非正兵，安能致远?偏箱、鹿角，兵之大要：一则治力，一则

【今译】

法，现在征讨高丽却说使用正规战法，这是什么原因?”

李靖说：“诸葛亮七擒孟获，用的不是别的，正是正规的打法。”

太宗说：“西晋马隆讨伐凉州树机能的叛乱时，也是依照八阵图的做法，制造偏箱车。在地形开阔地带作战，则用鹿角车摆成八阵实施攻击；在路面狭窄地方行军作战，则把木屋放在偏箱车上，一边战斗一边前进。可以肯定，正规的战法是古人所重视的。”

李靖说：“臣讨伐突厥时，西行数千里。如果不是用正规的方法怎么能从事这样的远征呢?使用偏箱车、鹿角车在军事上的重要意义是：一可以掌握我方部队的战斗力，二可以阻挡敌人前来冲击，

(Tu chueh), you used unorthodox tactics. Now you are going to apply orthodox tactics against Gaoli troops, can you tell me why?"

Li Jing said: "When Zhuge Liang captured Meng Huo seven times, he used no other tactics than orthodox ones. That's it."

Tang Taizong said: "When Ma Long of the Western Jin Dynasty conducted a punitive campaign against Shu Jineng's rebellion in Liang Zhou, he also employed the 'Diagram of Eight Formations' and built the narrow chariots. When the terrain was broad, he deployed the 'deer horn chariots' in eight formations to conduct the attack; when the road was narrow, he placed wooden huts on the narrow chariots and advanced while fighting. I believe that it was orthodox tactics that the ancients valued!"

Li Jing said: "When I conducted the punitive campaign against the Turks, we traveled west for several thousand li. If we had not employed orthodox tactics, how could we have gone so far? The importance in military operations to use narrow chariots and deer horn chariots is that in the first place, it helps us to be aware of our capability; in the second, it provides a defense a-

【原文】

前拒，一则束部伍，三者迭相为用。斯马隆所得古法深矣！”

太宗曰：“朕破宋老生，初交锋，义师少却。朕亲以铁骑自南原驰下，横突之，老生兵断后，大溃，遂擒之。此正兵乎，奇兵乎？”

靖曰：“陛下天纵圣武，非学而能。臣按兵法，自黄帝以来，先正而后奇，先仁义而后权谲。且霍

【今译】

三可以约束自己的队伍。这三种好处交相运用。由此可知马隆研究古人用兵方法达到了精深的地步！”

唐太宗说：“朕击破宋老生的那次战斗，两军刚刚交锋，我们右翼部队就稍向后退，不利。朕亲率精锐骑兵从南原急驰而下，从侧后突击宋老生军，宋老生的后路被切断，随即大败，于是活捉了宋老生。这是正兵呢，还是奇兵呢？”

李靖说：“陛下乃是天赋神武，这决不是凭后天学习可以获得的英明才干。臣按兵法所说，自从黄帝以来，用兵作战都是先用正兵，后用奇兵；先

gainst the enemy assaults; in the third, it helps to control our own troops. When being applied, these three will play their respective roles in turn. So we can see how thoroughly Ma Long learned these ancient strategies and tactics!"

Tang Taizong said: "At the battle in which I defeated Song Laosheng, the moment the fronts clashed, our right flank troops retreated slightly and the situation became unfavorable. I then led our elite cavalry in person to race down from the Southern Plain and made a flank attack on Song Laosheng's troops from behind and cut off their retreat. Then they were totally defeated and Song Laosheng was captured alive. Was this orthodox or unorthodox?"

Li Jing said: "Your Majesty's military talents are endowed by Heaven and can never be acquired by studying. Observing the military strategies as practiced from the Yellow Emperor on down, I find that the strategy applied was always orthodox first and unorthodox afterward, benevolence and righteousness first and scheming and cheating afterward. In the battle of Huo Yi, we launched the campaign out of righteousness, so it was orthodox. Jian Cheng fell off his

【原文】

邑之战，师以义举者，正也；建成坠马，右军少却者，奇也。”

太宗曰：“彼时少却，几败大事，曷谓奇邪？”

靖曰：“凡兵，以前向为正，后却为奇。且右军不却，则老生安致之来哉？《法》曰：‘利而诱之，乱而取之。’老生不知兵，恃勇急进，不意断后，见擒于陛下。此所谓以奇为正也。”

太宗曰：“霍去病暗与孙、吴合，诚有是夫！

【今译】

行仁义，后施权谋。霍邑之战，我军为正义而出师，就是正兵；建成在战场上落马，右翼部队稍向后退，这是奇兵。”

太宗说：“当时部队的后退，几乎坏了大事，怎么说它是出奇用兵呢？”

李靖说：“大凡用兵打仗，一般都以向前攻击为正兵，向后佯败退却为奇兵。如果右翼部队不退却，怎能诱致宋老生军贸然进击呢？《孙子兵法》说：‘利而诱之，乱而取之’（敌人贪利，就用小利引诱他；敌人混乱，就乘机攻取它），宋老生不懂用兵之法，依仗匹夫之勇就来进击，没想到后路会被截断，于是被陛下生擒。这就是所谓以奇为正。”

太宗说：“‘霍去病暗与孙、吴合’（霍去病没有读过兵书，但用兵作战的原则与《孙子》、《吴子》多能吻合），看来真有其事！当右翼部队后退时，高

horse in the battlefield and the right flank forces retreated slightly. This was unorthodox."

Tang Taizong said: "That slight retreat almost ruined the whole situation. how can you refer to it as an unorthodox tactic?"

Li Jing said: "In a battle, when troops advance to attack, it is orthodox; when they feign to retreat, it is unorthodox. If our right flank forces had not retreated, how could we have had Song Laosheng's troops to come forward rashly? *Sun Zi's Art of War* states: 'Entice the enemy if he is greedy; take him if he is disordered.' Song Laosheng did not know tactics of warfare. Because of his foolhardiness, he moved hastily forward and did not expect that his retreat could be cut off, and so was captured alive by Your Majesty. This is the so-called 'using the unorthodox as the orthodox.'"

Tang Taizong said: "It seems that what people said is true that 'Huo Qubing did not read any military books but his tactics unknowingly cohered with those of Sun Zi's and Wu Zi's.' When the right flank forces retreated, my father Gao Zu turned pale with fright. But when I succeeded in my forceful attack, the situation turned

【原文】

当石(右)军之却也，高祖失色，及朕奋击，反为我利。孙、吴暗合，卿实知言。”

太宗曰：“凡兵却皆谓之奇乎?”

靖曰：“不然。夫兵却，旗参差而不齐，鼓大小而不应，令喧嚣而不一，此真败却也，非奇也。若旗齐鼓应，号令如一，纷纷纭纭，虽退走，非败也，必有奇也。《法》曰：‘佯北勿追’，又曰：‘能而示之不能’，皆奇之谓也。”

太宗曰：“霍邑之战，右军少却，其天乎？老生被擒，其人乎?”

【今译】

祖大惊失色，等到朕奋力突击得手后，反而造成我方十分有利的形势。这也是‘暗与孙、吴合’，爱卿分析得很有见地。”

太宗说：“大凡军队退却，都能说是奇兵吗?”

李靖说：“不是的。部队退却时，假如旗帜参差不齐，鼓声有大有小不能相互呼应，号令喧嚣而不统一，这是真正的败退之兵，而非奇兵。如果旗帜整齐，鼓声呼应，号令如一，表面上看人马纷纭，似乱不乱，即使他们是在退走，也不是真的败退，其中必然有奇。《孙子兵法》说：‘佯北勿追’(敌军佯败不要追击)，又说：‘能而示之不能’(能打，装作不能打)，这都是用奇的论述。”

太宗说：“霍邑之战，右军稍退，这是天意吗？宋老生被活捉，这是人的力量使然吗?”

to be advantageous for us. This is also an 'unknowingly cohering with Sun Zi's and Wu Zi's tactics.' Sure you are good at these words."

Tang Taizong said: "Whenever an army retreats, can we say that it is an unorthodox tactic?"

Li Jing said: "We can not say so. When an army retreats, if its flags are confused and disordered, its drums sound loud and low not responding to each other and orders are shouted in a clamor, then it is a true retreat in defeat and not an unorthodox tactic. If the flags are in good order, the sound of drums responds to each other and the commands and orders are integrated, although it looks like that they are retreating in a rush and disorder, it is not a retreat in defeat but very possibly an unorthodox tactic. *Sun Zi's Art of War* says: 'Do not pursue the retreat in feigned defeat.' It also says: 'Pretend to be not capable while capable.' All these are referred to as unorthodox."

Tang Taizong said: "At the Battle of Huo Yi, the right flank forces retreated slightly, was it decided by the will of Heaven? Song Laosheng was captured alive, was it due to the efforts of man?"

【原文】

靖曰："若非正兵变为奇，奇兵变为正，则安能胜哉？故善用兵者，奇正在人而已。变而神之，所以推乎天也。"

太宗俯首。

太宗曰："奇正素分之欤，临时制之欤？"

靖曰："按《曹公新书》曰：'己二而敌一，则一术为正，一术为奇；己五而敌一，则三术为正，二术为奇。'此言大略尔。唯孙武云：'战势不过奇正，奇正之变，不可胜穷。奇正相生，如循环之无

【今译】

李靖曰："如果不是陛下使正兵变为奇兵，奇兵变为正兵，那怎能打成胜仗呢？所以，对善于用兵的人来说，用奇还是用正，全在人的调度指挥而已。奇正变化达到神奇莫测、出神入化的地步，人们便把它归结为天意。"

太宗点头赞同。

唐太宗说："奇兵正兵是平时就截然分开的呢，还是到战场上才临时分派的呢？"

李靖说："按《曹公新书》的说法：'当我之兵力两倍于敌时，我就以一部为正兵，一部为奇兵；当我五倍于敌时，就以三成的兵力作正兵，二成的兵力作奇兵。'这只是大概的说法。只有孙武说的'作战的态势，不过是奇正罢了，但奇正的变化却是

Li Jing said: "If Your Majesty had not changed the orthodox force into unorthodox force and unorthodox force into orthodox force, how could the victory have been won? So, for a good commander, orthodox and unorthodox lie with his commands and directions. When the change of orthodox and unorthodox becomes unpredictable and reaches the height of perfection, people then will tend to attribute it to the will of Heaven."

Tang Taizong nodded in agreement.

Tang Taizong said: "Are the orthodox and unorthodox distinguished beforehand, or are they determined at the time of battle?"

Li Jing said: "According to the *New Book of Duke Cao*: 'If we outnumber the enemy two to one, then divide our forces into two sections, with one section being orthodox and the other being unorthodox; if we outnumber the enemy five to one, then three sections should be orthodox and two sections be unorthodox.' This is a rough explanation. Sun Wu said: 'The posture of warfare never exceeds unorthodox and orthodox but their changes will by no means be exhausted. The unorthodox and orthodox trans-

【原文】

端，孰能穷之?’斯得之矣，安有素分之邪？若士卒未习吾法，偏裨未熟吾令，则必为之二术。教战时，各认旗鼓，迭相分合，故曰：‘分合为变’，此教战之术尔。教阅既成，众知吾法，然后如驱群羊，由将所指，孰分奇正之别哉？孙武所谓‘形人而我无形’，此乃奇正之极致。是以素分者教阅也，临时制

【今译】

不可穷尽的。奇正相互转化，如同圆环没有末端一样，谁能穷尽它的奥妙?’这话才是真正说透了奇正的道理，哪有平时就区分奇正的呢？如果士卒没有学会我的战法，部将没有熟悉我的号令，那就要对他们教练奇正相变之术。训练教战时，要让各部队认别指挥的旗帜和鼓音，反复进行分散和集中的演练，这便是《孙子兵法》中说的‘分合为变’（按照分散和集中兵力来变换战术），这是平时训练部队学习奇正的方法。训练完成之后，部队上下都熟知我的套路，然后就能像驱赶羊群一样，听凭将帅指挥，谁还能分清是奇是正呢？孙武说的‘形人而我无形’（让敌人暴露真情而不让自己情况暴露），这是运用奇正所达到的最高境界。所以说，平时分别奇正，那只是训练之法，在战场上根据情况变化而

form themselves into each other, just like moving in a cycle, never coming to an end. Who can exhaust their changes?' These words have captured the beauty of unorthodox and orthodox. How can they be distinguished beforehand? If the officers and soldiers are not trained to learn my battle tactics, and if the assistant generals are not familiar with my commands and orders, then you have to teach them unorthodox and orthodox tactics as well as their mutual transformation. When learning battle tactics, the units should be trained separately or together time and again in order to let them be able to recognize the commands and orders by flags and sounds of drums. This is the so-called 'to change tactics by dividing and combining the forces' as in *Sun Zi's Art of War* and this is the way to train the troops to learn unorthodox and orthodox. When training is finished and all troops know my methods, they will be driven like a flock of sheep following the generals' commands. Who then can make a distinction of unorthodox and orthodox? Sun Wu said: 'Let the enemy expose and hide ourselves.' This is the pinnacle in employing unorthodox and orthodox. Therefore, a

【原文】

变者不可胜穷也。”

太宗曰：“深乎，深乎！曹公必知之矣。但《新书》所以授诸将而已，非奇正本法。”

太宗曰：“曹公云：‘奇兵旁击’，卿谓若何？”

靖曰：“臣按曹公注《孙子》曰：‘先出合战为正，后出为奇’，此与旁击之拘异焉。臣愚谓大众所合为正，将所自出为奇，乌有失(先)后旁击之拘哉？”

太宗曰：“吾之正，使敌视以为奇；吾之奇，

【今译】

活用奇正那是没有穷尽的啊。”

太宗说：“深奥啊，深奥啊！曹操必定是深知这些道理的。但是，《曹公新书》里的奇正之论只不过是为了教练诸将而已，还不是关于奇正的根本法则。”

太宗说：“曹操说：‘奇兵旁击’（奇兵就是从侧背打击敌人），你认为是怎样的？”

李靖说：“臣按曹操注《孙子》所说：‘先出合战为正，后出为奇’（率先同敌人交战的是正兵，尔后出击的部队是奇兵），这里讲的与‘奇兵旁击’的拘牵之说不同。我认为，主力同敌人交战就是正兵，将帅使用机动部队出击就是奇兵，哪里能拘泥于先击、后击与侧击的说法呢？”

太宗说：“我本来使用正兵，却能使敌人以为我在用奇兵；我本来使用奇兵，却能使敌人以为我

distinction beforehand is merely a way for training and application of unorthodox and orthodox according to the change of situation in the battlefield is quite inexhaustible."

Tang Taizong said: "Profound indeed! Cao Cao must have known all these very well. The statements about unorthodox and orthodox in the New Book of Duke Cao are made only for the training of the generals, they are not laws of unorthodox and orthodox."

Tang Taizong said: "Cao Cao said: 'Unorthodox tactics is to attack from the flank.' What do you think about this?"

Li Jing said: "I recall that Cao Cao said in his annotation of *Sun Zi's Art of War* that 'those troops who engage the enemy first are orthodox troops; those who attack afterward are unorthodox troops.' This is different from the statement that 'unorthodox tactics is to attack from the flank.' In my opinion, when main force is used to engage the enemy, it is orthodox; while when reserved force is used, it is unorthodox. How should one stick fast to first attack, later attack and flank attack?"

Tang Taizong said: "If I make the enemy

【原文】

使敌视以为正，斯所谓‘形人者’欤？以奇为正，以正为奇，变化莫测，斯所谓‘无形者’欤？”

靖再拜曰：“陛下神圣，迥出古人，非臣所及。”

太宗曰：“分合为变者，奇正安在？”

靖曰：“善用兵者，无不正，无不奇，使敌莫测。故正亦胜，奇亦胜。三军之士，止知其胜，莫

【今译】

在用正兵，这就是所谓的‘形人’吗？以奇为正，以正为奇，变化莫测，这就是所谓的‘无形’吗？”

李靖再拜，说：“陛下神智圣武，实在远超古人，更不是臣等所能企及的。”

太宗说：“部队在战场上分合变化时，奇正表现在哪里呢？”

李靖说：“善于用兵的人，无处不是正兵，无处不是奇兵，使敌人无法测知。所以，用正兵也能取胜，用奇兵也能取胜。全军上下，只知道打了胜仗，但不知是怎样打胜的。若不是把奇兵正兵的变

take my orthodox as unorthodox and my unorthodox as orthodox, is it the so-called 'let the enemy expose himself'? If unorthodox is used as orthodox and orthodox used as unorthodox with unfathomable changes and transformations, is this what is meant by 'hide ourselves'?"

Li Jing bowed again and said: "Your Majesty's wisdom and military talents really exceed the ancients and are quite beyond what I can attain."

Tang Taizong said: "When the forces are changing by dividing and combining in the battlefield, how can unorthodox and orthodox be discerned?"

Li Jing said: "For a good commander, there are none that are not orthodox and none that are not unorthodox, so the enemy will never be sure. Thus you can win with the orthodox and you can also win with the unorthodox. The officers and soldiers throughout the army only know that they have won but never know how they won. Without being so skilful at employing the changes and transformations of the unorthodox and orthodox, how can such a good effect be produced? Only Sun Wu was capable of com-

【原文】

知其所以胜。非变而能通，安能至是哉？分合所出，唯孙武能之。吴起而下，莫可及焉。”

太宗曰：“吴术若何？”

靖曰：“臣请略言之。魏武侯问吴起两军相向，起曰：‘使贱而勇者前击，锋始交而北，北而勿罚，观敌进取。一坐一起，奔北不追，则敌有谋矣；若悉众追北，行止纵横，此敌人不才，击之勿疑。’臣

【今译】

化运用到非常娴熟精通的境地，怎么能有这么好的效果？分合变化、奇正相生的奥妙玄机，只有孙武能够做到，吴起以下没有人能赶得上他。”

太宗说：“吴起用兵的方法是怎样的？”

李靖说：“请允许我大概地讲一下。魏武侯问吴起，两军相向时怎样才能了解对方将领的用兵才能？吴起回答说：‘让地位卑微而勇敢的军官带部队向前出击，刚一交锋时就要败退下来。对败退下来的部队不制止、不怪罪，目的在于察看敌人的进攻情势。如果敌人或进或止都很有节制，对我败退下来的队伍也不追击，这就说明敌方将领很有头脑；如果敌人倾全力追击我方败退下来的队伍，并且秩序混乱，这就说明敌方将领胸无韬略，可立即进攻他，不必迟疑。’我认为，吴起的战法大都是这样

prehending the profundity and mystery of the change of dividing and combining and the mutual transformation of unorthodox and orthodox. From Wu Qi on, no one has been able to catch up with him."

Tang Taizong said: "What was Wu Qi's operational strategy like?"

Li Jing said: "Please permit me to give a general account. Marquis Wu of Wei asked Wu Qi: 'How do you get to know about the military capability of the general of the opposite side when the two armies confront each other?' Wu Qi replied: 'Have some low-ranking but courageous officers lead their men to go forward and attack. They will flee the moment they engage the enemy. You are not to stop and blame the fleeing forces so as to observe the advancing posture of the enemy. If their advancing and halting are under good control and they do not pursue your fleeing troops, then it means that the enemy general is very resourceful; if they go all out to pursue your fleeing troops and in disordered fashion, it then means that the enemy general is not a strategist and not talented, so you can attack him without hesitation.' I think that

【原文】

谓吴术大率多此类，非孙武所谓以正合也。”

太宗曰：“卿舅韩擒虎尝言，卿可与论孙、吴，亦奇正之谓乎?”

靖曰：“擒虎安知奇正之极，但以奇为奇，以正为正尔！曾未知奇正相变，循环无穷者也。”

太宗曰：“古人临阵出奇，攻人不意，斯亦相变之法乎?”

靖曰：“前代战斗，多是以小术而胜无术，以

【今译】

的，并不是孙武所说的用正兵和敌人交战。”

太宗说：“爱卿的舅舅韩擒虎曾经说，只有你能够和他探讨孙武、吴起的兵法。你们讨论的也就是奇正变化的奥秘吗?”

李靖说：“我的舅舅韩擒虎哪里懂得奇正变化的奥妙，仅仅是知道奇兵就是奇兵、正兵就是正兵罢了，连奇正相变、循环无穷的道理都不知道。”

唐太宗说：“古人临阵出奇，攻敌不意，这也是奇正相互变化的法则吗?”

李靖说：“先前的战斗，大多都是有一点谋略的人战胜没有谋略的人，懂得一点用兵之道的人战

Wu Qi's strategy is generally of this sort, not the 'orthodox engagement' as referred to by Sun Wu."

Tang Taizong said: "Your uncle Han Qinhu once said that only you could discuss Sun Wu's and Wu Qi's operational art with him. Is the secrecy of the changes of the unorthodox and orthodox what you discussed?"

Li Jing said: "How could my uncle Han Qinhu know the secrecy of the changes of the unorthodox and orthodox? What he knows is only that the unorthodox is the unorthodox and the orthodox is the orthodox. He even does not know that unorthodox and orthodox can change and transform into each other and the changes will circulate and are inexhaustible."

Tang Taizong said: "When the ancients approached the enemy formations, they would send forth unorthodox forces to take the enemy by surprise. Was this also a law of the mutual changing and transforming of unorthodox and orthodox?"

Li Jing said: "In battles of the earlier ages, the fact was always that men who were able to

【原文】

片善而胜无善，斯安足以论兵法也？若谢玄之破苻坚，非谢玄之善也，盖苻坚之不善也。”

太宗顾侍臣检《谢玄传》，阅之曰：“苻坚甚处是不善？”

靖曰：“臣观《苻坚载记》曰：秦诸军皆溃败，唯慕容垂一军独全。坚以千余骑赴之，垂子宝劝垂杀坚，不果。此有以见秦师之乱。慕容垂独全，盖

【今译】

胜用兵无方的人，这些人哪里谈得上讨论兵法呢？比如东晋的谢玄大破前秦的苻坚，并非谢玄善于用兵，而是苻坚不会用兵罢了。”

太宗让侍臣找出《谢玄传》，阅读之后说：“苻坚用兵有哪些不当之处呢？”

李靖说：“臣读《苻坚载记》，书上说：淝水之战，前秦诸军都溃败了，唯有慕容垂一军完好无损。苻坚曾率领败军千余骑投奔他，慕容垂的儿子慕容宝却劝他杀苻坚自立，后来此事没成。从这儿可以看到前秦军队的内部是多么混乱。慕容垂一军独全，

devise a stratagem would defeat those who were not able to do that and those who had some knowledge about military tactics would defeat those who did not have any such knowledge. How could they be qualified to discuss the art of war? For example, Xie Xuan of Eastern Jin completely defeated Fu Jian of Former Qin not because Xie Xuan was good at military tactics but because Fu Jian was not good at it."

Tang Taizong ordered his attending officer to find *Xie Xuan's Biography* and said after having read it: "What then is wrong with Fu Jian's strategy?"

Li Jing said: " I observe that *Fu Jian's Biography* records that at the Battle of Fei Shui all armies of Former Qin had been defeated and had fled with only Mu Rongchui's army left intact. Fu Jian went to join him with some one thousand remaining cavalry. Mu Rongchui's son Mu Rongbao persuaded him to kill Fu Jian but without result. From this, one can see what a confusion they had there in Former Qin's armies. Only Mu Rongchui's army remained intact, so it is obvious that Fu Jian had been set up by Murong Chui. Now to be set up by your own people and

【原文】

坚为垂所陷明矣。夫为人所陷而欲胜敌，不亦难乎？臣故曰无术焉，苻坚之类是也。”

太宗曰：“《孙子》谓多算胜少算，有以知少算胜无算。凡事皆然。”

太宗曰：“黄帝兵法，世传《握奇文》，或谓为《握机文》，何谓也？”

靖曰：“奇，音机，故或传为机，其义则一。考其词云：‘四为正，四为奇，余奇为握机。’奇，余

【今译】

显见苻坚是受了慕容垂的陷害。受自己人陷害，还想在战场上打败敌人，这不是很难办吗？臣因此说用兵没有谋略的就是苻坚这样的一类人。”

太宗说：“《孙子兵法》说计算周密、取胜条件充分的，就能打败计算疏漏、取胜条件不足的；据此可以推知，计算疏漏、取胜条件不足的，可以打败毫无成算、毫无取胜条件的。一切事情都是这个道理。”

唐太宗说：“黄帝的兵法，按后世传说称为《握奇文》，或者称作《握机文》，究竟叫什么？”

李靖说：“‘奇’，读音为‘机’，所以也将‘奇’传为‘机’，它们意义相同。考察书中的话，四方为正兵，四隅为奇兵，中央的余奇之兵即为主将掌握的机动部队。所谓‘奇’，是剩余的意思，因而‘奇’

still hope to defeat the enemy, isn't it too difficult a job to do? Thus I say that men like Fu Jian are those who know nothing about strategy."

Tang Taizong said: "Sun Zi said in his *Art of War* that those who calculate extensively with good scores can defeat those who calculate less with bad scores; those who calculate less with bad scores would defeat those who never calculate with no score at all. All things go like this."

Tang Taizong said: "The Yellow Emperor's art of war has been transmitted to later generations as *The Classic of Holding the Unorthodox or The Classic of Holding the Opportunity.* Which of these titles is correct?"

Li Jing said: "The pronunciation of the character 'unorthodox' is the same as that for 'opportunity,' so 'unorthodox' has been transmitted as 'opportunity,' but here the meaning is the same. If we examine the book, we can find it saying: 'Those that are deployed in the four directions are orthodox forces; those that are deployed in the four corners are unorthodox forces; the odd remaining forces deployed in the center are reserved forces held by the chief commanding general.' Here, 'unorthodox' means 'odd'

【原文】

零也，因此音机。臣愚谓兵无不是机，安在乎握而言也?当为余奇则是。夫正兵受之于君，奇兵将所自出。《法》曰：‘令素行以教其民，则民服。’此受之于君者也。又曰：‘兵不豫言，君命有所不受。’此将所自出者也。凡将，正而无奇，则守将也；奇

【今译】

读音同‘机’。臣以为，战场上战机无处不在，哪里有什么专门掌握的战机呢？应当理解为掌握中军机动部队并随机应变才对。一般来说执行国君总的战略意图为正兵，将领按战场情况灵活使用兵力是奇兵。《孙子兵法》说：‘令素行以教其民，则民服。’（平时就教育士卒做到令行禁止，士卒就能养成服从命令的习惯）这是指按照君主命令行事的正兵。《孙子兵法》又说：‘兵不豫言，君命有所不受。’（用兵作战的具体打法不能在战前刻板规定。即使是国君的命令，如果不符合战场变化了的情况，那也应当有所变通，甚至可不接受）这是指将领临机决断、灵活使用兵力。大凡将领，只会用正不会用奇的，那是墨守陈规的将领；只会用奇而不会用正的，那是浮躁好斗的将领；既会用正又会用奇的，那是国家栋梁。所以说，掌握战机必须使用机动兵

and is pronounced the same as 'opportunity.' In my opinion, since there is nothing in the battlefield that is not an opportunity, then is there anything one should always hold as an opportunity? So 'holding the opportunity' ought to be understood as sustaining the reserved forces in the center to cope with the changing odds. Generally speaking, orthodox forces are those forces deployed according to the ruler's strategic intention, and unorthodox forces are those that can be deployed and employed by generals in accordance with the changing situation of the battlefield. *Sun Zi's Art of War* says: 'If orders are consistently carried out and troops are strictly supervised in peace time, then they will be obedient.' This is said for the orthodox forces which carry out the ruler's orders. *Sun Zi's Art of War* also says: 'Tactics should not be decided beforehand. Even the ruler's orders, if they are not fit to the changed situation of the battlefield, may have to be altered or even disobeyed.' This is said to mean that generals should make their decisions according to the circumstances and be flexible in using their forces. As for generals, if they can only apply orthodox tactics and never

【原文】

而无正，则斗将也；奇正皆得，国之辅也。是故握机握奇，本无二法，在学者兼通而已。”

太宗曰：“阵数有九，中心零者，大将握之，四面八向，皆取准焉。阵间容阵，队间容队。以前为后，以后为前。进无速奔，退无遽走。四头八尾，

【今译】

力，掌握机动兵力必须善于抓住战机，二者不能截然分开，关键在于学习者能否融会贯通罢了。”

太宗说：“(八阵中) 区分为九个小方阵，(外围有四正四奇)，中央一阵为余零之兵，由大将掌握。四方四隅各阵都向中阵看齐取准。大阵之中包容许多小阵，大部队之中包容许多小分队。可以以前阵为后阵，也可以把后阵变为前阵。前进时不快跑，后退时不急走。整个方阵四头八尾，哪部分受

use unorthodox ones, they are sticklers for conventions; if they can only apply unorthodox tactics and never use orthodox ones, they are but impetuous and bellicose generals; only those who can use both orthodox and unorthodox tactics are pillars of the state. Thus if you want to grasp the opportunity for battle, you must use the reserved forces and if you want to use the reserved forces, you must be good at grasping the opportunities. These two can not be separated. To learn to be good at both of them, one must have a thorough understanding of the inherent relations between them."

Tang Taizong said: "(Within the eight formations), there are nine small phalanxes (with four orthodox and four unorthodox in the periphery), the central phalanx is formed by the remaining odd forces under the direct command of the chief general. The phalanxes in the four directions and four corners orient themselves to the central phalanx. Within the large phalanxes, small phalanxes are contained; within the big arrays, small arrays are contained. The front can be used as the rear and the rear as the front. When advancing, they do not run quickly; when

【原文】

触处为首，敌冲其中，两头皆救。数起于五，而终于八，此何谓也？”

靖曰：“诸葛亮以石纵横布为八行，方阵之法即此图也。臣尝教阅，必先此阵。世所传《握机文》，盖得其粗也。”

太宗曰：“天、地、风、云，龙、虎、鸟、蛇，斯八阵何义也？”

靖曰：“传之者误也。古人秘藏此法，故诡设八名尔。八阵本一也，分为八焉。若天、地者，本乎旗号；风、云者，本乎幡名；龙、虎、鸟、蛇者，

【今译】

到攻击，哪部分立即变为阵首迎击。如果敌人冲击中阵，那么方阵头尾皆来救应。布阵的数目最初是五个，而后演变为八个，这是什么道理呢？”

李靖说：“诸葛亮用石块纵横排列八行，八阵的布阵方法正和这个阵图一样。我过去教练部队阵法，总是先教会他们此阵。现今世上所传《握机文》，只不过是说明了一些梗概罢了。”

唐太宗说：“天、地、风、云，龙、虎、鸟、蛇，这八个阵的含义是什么？”

李靖说：“这是后人讹传发生的错误。古人为了对这一阵法保密，故意安排了八个神秘名字。其实八阵本是一个阵，分为八个部分罢了。比如天、地和风、云，都是几种幡旗的名号；龙、虎、鸟、

withdrawing, they do not race off. The whole formation has four heads and eight tails. Whichever part of it is struck, that part will immediately become the head. If the enemy attacks the middle, then the head and tail of the struck formation will come to the rescue. Originally, the number of the phalanx was five and evolved finally into eight. What does this mean?"

Li Jing said: "Zhuge Liang set stones out horizontally and vertically to make eight rows. The configuration of the eight formations is based on this formation diagram. When I taught troops formations in the past, I invariably began with this formation. What has been passed down as *The Classics of Holding the Opportunity* only includes a rough outline of it."

Tang Taizong said: "Heaven, Earth, wind, cloud, dragon, tiger, bird, snake, what is the meaning of these eight formations?"

Li Jing said: "An error occurred when they were being passed down. In order to keep a secret of them, the ancients created eight names for them on purpose. In fact, the eight formations originally were one divided into eight parts. For example, Heaven, Earth, wind and

【原文】

本乎队伍之别。后世误传。诡设物象，何止八而已乎？”

太宗曰：“数起于五，而终于八，则非设象，实古制也。卿试陈之。”

靖曰：“臣按黄帝始立丘井之法，因以制兵。故井分四道，八家处之，其形井字，开方九焉。五为阵法，四为闲地，此所谓数起于五也；虚其中，

【今译】

蛇，本来是各个部队的序列之别。后来的人辗转相传发生错误。如果各个大阵小阵都要以各种物象命名，那又何止八种呢？”

太宗说：“布阵的数目开始是五个，最后推演为八个，不是由于假设物象的缘故，而是古代的一种传统制度。你可以详细谈一谈。”

李靖说：“臣按黄帝创立的丘井之法，用它确立兵制。一‘井’有四条相交大道，八家共处一‘井’，土地的形状像‘井’字，正好分成九个方块。以井田比喻八阵，则前、后、左、右、中即为五块阵地，余下东南、西南、西北、东北四块闲地，这就是所谓布阵之数从五开始；空出中央阵地，由大

cloud were names for flags and dragon, tiger, bird and snake originated in the distinctions of various arrays. Later, when they were passed down there occurred an error. If it were a must that all the big and small phalanxes be named after images, why should they have stopped just at eight?"

Tang Taizong said: "The number of the formation began with five and then evolved into eight. If they were not set up as images, then they must reflect an ancient tradition. Would you explain that for me?"

Li Jing said: "I established the combat system based on the method of 'well' created by the Yellow Emperor. A well is formed of four crossing roads and eight families are located around one well. The character 井(well) originated from such a configuration and is divided into just nine squares. To compare the eight formations with this character, we can see that there are front, rear, left, right and central squares for the five positions with the southeastern, southwestern, northwestern and northeastern squares open for allocation. This is the reason why the number of formations began with five. The central was left

【原文】

大将居之，环其四面，诸部连绕，此所谓终于八也。及乎变化制敌，则纷纷纭纭，斗乱而法不乱；混混沌沌，形圆而势不散：此所谓散而成八，复而为一者也。”

太宗曰：“深乎，黄帝之制兵也！后世虽有天智神略，莫能出其斗(阃)阈。降此孰有继之者乎？”

靖曰：“周之始兴，则太公实缮其法：始于岐

【今译】

将居中指挥，各部四隅环绕列阵，布阵之数就演变为八阵了。到了变换队形打击敌人的时候，部队频繁机动，旌旗招展，虽然阵地上纷乱厮杀，阵法却不错乱；战车奔驰，车毂相击，刀光交错，寒光闪闪，阵形浑圆而阵势不散。这就是所谓各阵散开作战可以分成八小阵，各阵联合起来作战是一个大阵。”

太宗说：“多么深奥啊，黄帝所创制的兵法！后人即使有很高的智慧、很深的谋略，也没能超出他的思想。黄帝之后有谁称得上是继承了黄帝兵法的呢？”

李靖说：“西周刚刚兴起的时候，姜太公曾整理过黄帝兵法，开始在岐都建立井田制度，拥有战

open for the chief general to command the formations. With the commander's position unchanged and formations placed in the four corners around, the number of the formations then becomes eight. When attacking the enemy with changed formations, the arrays will move frequently with flags flapping to and fro. Though the fighting is fierce, the formation is not disordered. Chariots are racing, wheels are clashing, swords are glinting and flashing, but the formation is intact and its power is not dispersed. That is what is meant when we say that the formation can be dispersed into eight small ones and reunited into a big one."

Tang Taizong said: "How profound was the military art created by the Yellow Emperor! Even if the later generations have men with great wisdom and planning ability, none has exceeded his thinking. Then after the Yellow Emperor, who can be said to be a successor to his art?"

Li Jing said: "When the Western Zhou Dynasty was first established, Jiang Taigong had worked on the Yellow Emperor's military art and started to establish the 'nine square system'

【原文】

都，以建井亩；戎车三百辆，虎贲三千人，以立军制，六步七步，六伐七伐，以教战法。陈师牧野，太公以百夫致师，以成武功，以四万五千人胜纣七十万众。周《司马法》，本太公者也。太公既没，齐人得其遗法。至桓公霸天下，任管仲，复修太公法，谓之节制之师。诸侯毕服。”

太宗曰：“儒者多言管仲霸臣而已，殊不知兵

【今译】

车三百辆、虎贲三千人，创立西周军制，教练时以六步七步、六伐七伐教会作战方法。牧野一战，姜太公挑选百名勇士为前锋，率先冲击敌阵，成就武功，取得了四万五千人大胜商纣七十万军队的战绩。周代兵书《司马法》是基于太公兵法而作的。太公去世以后，齐国人得到其遗传的兵法。到齐桓公称霸天下时，任用管仲为相，重新整理太公兵法，使齐国的军队成为纪律严明、训练有素的军队，天下诸侯没有不畏服的。”

太宗说：“一般学者都说管仲是个以霸道治天下的谋臣，殊不知其兵法却是以王者制度为基础的。

in Qi Du. With three hundred chariots and three thousand Tiger Warriors, he established the military organization of Western Zhou and taught them battle tactics by practicing six paces and seven paces and six attacks and seven attacks. At the battle of Mu Ye, Jiang Taigong selected a hundred warriors as the vanguard to punch the enemy formations, established his military merit and achieved a complete victory with forty-five thousand men against the seven hundred thousand troops of King Zhou of Shang. The military book *The Methods of the "Sima"* of the Zhou Dynasty was written on the basis of Taigong's strategies. When Taigong died, people of Qi State obtained his bequeathed strategies. When Duke Huan of Qi became hegemon over all the other states, he appointed Guan Zhong as his prime minister, rearranged Taigong's strategies and made the army of Qi a strictly-disciplined and well-trained army. Then none of the feudal lords under Heaven dared not submit."

Tang Taizong said " Generally, scholars would consider Guan Zhong as a braintruster who assisted to rule All Under Heaven based on hegemony but they do not know that his military

【原文】

法乃本于王制也。诸葛亮王佐之才，自比管、乐，以此知管仲亦王佐也。但周衰时，王不能用，故假齐兴师尔。”

靖再拜曰：“陛下神圣，知人如此，老臣虽死，无愧昔贤也。臣请言管仲制齐之法：三分齐国，以为三军；五家为轨，故五人为伍；十轨为里，故五十人为小戎；四里为连，故二百人为卒；十连为乡，

【今译】

诸葛亮是辅弼帝王的贤能之才，喜欢以管仲、乐毅自况，从这里可知管仲也是辅佐帝王的贤才。但在周室衰微的时候，周王不能用他，所以只好凭借齐国的力量兴师匡正天下。”

李靖两次拜敬说：“陛下圣明，了解人如此深刻，老臣有幸躬逢圣朝，即使死去也无愧于先贤了。请让我讲一下管仲治理齐国的方法。他把齐国民众分为三部分，建立三军。行政上五家组成一轨，所以军制上五人组成一伍；行政上十轨组成一里，所以军制上五十人组成一小戎；行政上四里为一连，所以军制上二百人组成一卒；行政上十连为一乡，

strategies were based upon monarchy. Zhuge Liang was a worthy sustainer of the monarch. He often compared himself to Guan Zhong and Yue Yi. From this, we can see that Guan Zhong was also a worthy sustainer of a monarch. But when the Zhou Dynasty was declining, the king of Zhou could not use him, so he had to rely on the forces of Qi to restore orders under Heaven."

Li Jing bowed his head again and said: "Your Majesty is holy great and has such keen perception about people. I feel so lucky to have a chance to serve Your Majesty's government that even if I should die, I would not be ashamed before any of the previous great Worthies. Please allow me to say something about Gaun Zhong's way of governing Qi State. He divided the masses of Qi into three groups as three armies. The actual way is that as five families comprised an administrative organization of '*gui,*' so five men made up a military unit of '*wu*'; ten '*gui*' comprised an administrative '*li,*' so fifty men made up a military 'small rong'; four '*li*' comprised an administrative '*lian,*' so two hundred men made up a military '*zu*'; ten '*lian*' comprised an administrative '*xiang,*' so two thou-

【原文】

故二千人为旅；五乡一帅(师)，故万人为军。亦由《司马法》一帅(师)五旅，一旅五卒之义焉。其实皆得太公之遗法。”

太宗曰：“《司马法》人言穰苴所述，是欤，否也?”

靖曰：“按《史记·穰苴传》，齐景公时，穰苴善用兵，败燕晋之师，景公尊为司马之官，由是称司马穰苴，子孙号司马氏。至齐威王，追论古司马

【今译】

所以军制上二千人组成一旅；行政上五乡为一师，所以军制上一万人组成一军。这也是根据《司马法》所确定的军制，一个师下面分为五个旅，一个旅下面分为五个卒。其实，这些都来源于太公遗传下来的兵法。”

太宗说：“人们常说《司马法》是司马穰苴的著述，这种说法对还是不对?”

李靖说：“根据《史记·穰苴传》记载，齐景公时期，田穰苴善于用兵，曾打败燕晋之师，齐景公授予他司马这样的高官，从此人们称他为司马穰苴，子孙也称作司马氏。到齐威王时，人们追述探讨古代的司马兵法，同时也研究穰苴的军事论述，于是

sand men made up a military brigade; five '*xiang*' comprised an administrative '*shi,*' so ten thousand men made up a military corps. This is just like the military organization recorded in *The Methods of the "Sima"*: one division is divided into five brigades and one brigade into five '*zu.*' As a matter of fact, all these originated from Taigong's bequeathed strategies."

Tang Taizong said: "People often say that *The Methods of the Sima* was composed on the narration of Sima Rangju's. Is this true or not?"

Li Jing said: "According to the 'Biography of Rangju' in the *Shi Ji* (*Records of the Historian*), Tian Ranju excelled in commanding the army at the time of Duke Jing of Qi State and defeated the armies of the states of Yan and Jin, so he was given the rank of Sima (minister of war) by Duke Jing of Qi. From then on, he was called Sima Ranju and his sons and grandsons were also surnamed Sima. At the time of King Wei of Qi, people started to go back through the ancient Sima's art of war and at the same time began to study Rangju's military expositions which resulted in a book of dozens of chapters

【原文】

法，又述穰苴所学，遂有《司马穰苴书》数十篇。今世所传兵家流，又分权谋、形势、阴阳、技巧四种，皆出《司马法》也。”

太宗曰：“‘汉张良、韩信序次兵法，凡百八十二家，删取要用，定著三十五家。’今失其传，何也？”

靖曰：“张良所学，太公《六韬》、《三略》是也。韩信所学，穰苴、孙武是也。然大体不出三门四种而已。”

太宗曰：“何谓‘三门’？”

靖曰：“臣按：《太公·谋》八十一篇，所谓阴

【今译】

有《司马穰苴书》数十篇。现在流传下来的军事学派，分为兵权谋家、兵形势家、兵阴阳家、兵技巧家四种，其实都源出自《司马法》。”

太宗说：“‘汉初张良、韩信整理和编次当时的存世兵书，一共得到一百八十二家，经筛选取舍，定为三十五家。’（《汉书·艺文志·兵家》）现在这些兵书大都失传了，是怎么回事？”

李靖说：“张良学习的，是太公的《六韬》和《三略》；韩信学习的，是司马穰苴和孙武的军事学说。而这些古代兵书的类别，大体不外乎三门四种。”

太宗说：“什么叫做‘三门’？”

李靖说：“臣认为：《太公·谋》有八十一篇，所讲的‘阴谋’不是《太公·言》能够说明的。《太

called the *Book of Sima Ranju*. The military schools passed down to the present are divided into four categories which are the ' school of plotting and scheming,' the 'school of disposition and power,' the 'school of *Yin and Yang*' and the 'school of techniques and skills.' They all originate from *The Methods of the "Sima*."

Tang Taizong said: "At the beginning of the Han Dynasty, Zhang Liang and Han Xin assorted and compiled the then existing military books and divided them into one hundred and eighty-two schools. After strict screening and selection, they settled on thirty-five. Nowadays, most of the military books are lost when being passed down, how did this happen?"

Li Jing said: "What Zhang Liang studied was Taigong's *Six Stratagies* and *Three Strategems*. What Han Xin studied was the military doctrines of Sima Rangju's and Sun Wu's. All these ancient military books can be divided, in general, into three categories and four types."

Tang Taizong said: "What are the three categories?"

Li Jing said: "I think that there are eighty-one chapters in *The Plottings of Taigong* and the

【原文】

谋，不可以言穷；《太公·言》七十一篇，不可以兵穷；《太公·兵》八十五篇，不可以财穷。此三门也。"

太宗曰："何谓'四种'？"

靖曰："汉任宏所论是也。凡兵家流，权谋为一种，形势为一种，及阴阳、技巧二种，此四种也。"

太宗曰："《司马法》首序蒐狩，何也？"

靖曰："顺其时而要之以神，重其事也。《周

【今译】

公·言》有七十一篇，所讲的意义不是《太公·兵》能够说明的。《太公·兵》有八十五篇，所讲的意义不是用富国之道能够说明的。这就是'三门'。"

太宗说："什么叫做'四种'？"

李靖说："汉成帝时任宏论述了这个问题。他把兵家学派分成为：权谋是一种，形势是一种，以及阴阳、技巧两种，这就是'四种'。"

太宗说："《司马法》首先论述蒐狩田猎，为什么？"

李靖说："顺应农闲时节进行田猎以教练战法，并将所获猎物祭祀宗庙，托神明庇佑，这是表示对武备的重视。《周礼》一书把田猎视为最重要的制

'secret plottings' stated in it can not be explained by *The Sayings of Taigong*. There are seventy-one chapters in *The Sayings of Taigong* and what is talked about in it can not be explained by The Warfare of Taigong. There are eighty-five chapters in The Warfare of Taigong and what is talked about in it can not be explained by the way to prosper a state. These are the three categories."

Tang Taizong said: "Then what are the four types?"

Li Jing said: "Ren Hong discussed this at the time of Emperor Cheng of the Han Dynasty. He divided the schools of military strategists into the following types: Plotting and Scheming is one type, Disposition and Power is one type, Yin and Yang and Techniques and Skills are two types. These are the four types."

Tang Taizong said: "Why does *The Methods of the Sima* begin with the hunts?"

Li Jing said: "To seize the slack seasons of farming to teach battle tactics by means of hunting and offer the preys at the ancestral shrine so as to attain blessing from gods shows the stress laid on military preparations. In the book of

【原文】

礼》最为大政：成有岐阳之蒐，康有酆宫之朝，穆有涂山之会，此天子之事也。及周衰，齐桓有召陵之师，晋文有践土之盟，此诸侯奉行天子之事也。其实用九伐之法以威不恪。假之以朝会，因之以巡狩，训之以甲兵，言无事兵不妄举，必于农隙，不忘武备也。故首序蒐狩，不其深乎！”

太宗曰：“春秋楚子二广之法云：‘百官象物

【今译】

度，记录了周成王有岐阳之蒐，周康王有酆宫之朝，周穆王有涂山之会，这些是天子分内应做的事情。到周室衰微后，齐桓公有召陵之师，晋文公有践土之盟，这些是诸侯假借天子之命做的事情。这些做法实际上是用‘九伐之法’来威慑不听王命的诸侯，只是假借了朝会的名义，利用了巡猎的机会，进行了军事训练，旨在强调天下无事不可妄启干戈。田猎之所以在农闲时进行，这是不忘武备的表现啊。可见，《司马法》首先论述田猎，它的用意不是很深远吗?”

唐太宗说：“春秋时，楚庄王二广之法说：‘各级军官按照旌旗的指令而动，军队不待指令就作

Rites of Zhou, hunting is considered one of the most important regulations. It records the hunting at Qi Yang by King Chen of Zhou, the court assembly at Feng Palace by King Kang of Zhou and the meeting at Mount Tu by King Mu of Zhou, all these are what the Sons of Heaven should do. When Zhou's rule declined, Duke Huan of Qi assembled the armies at Zhao Ling and Duke Wen of Jin made his alliance at Jian Tu. All these were conducted by the feudal lords in the name of the Son of Heaven. In actuality, their purpose was to use the Law of Nine Punitive Expeditions to deter those feudal lords who dared to disobey the King's orders. They used the hunt to conduct military training under the pretext of the court assembly, warning the lords that no force should be used unless there was a need. That the hunts were held at the slack seasons of farming showed that they had not forgotten military preparations. Thus, is it profound that *The Methods of The "Sima"* begins with hunts?"

Tang Taizong said: "During the Spring and Autumn Period, in his Methods of Double

【原文】

而动，军政不戒而备。’此亦得周制欤？”

靖曰：“按左氏说，楚子乘广三十乘，广有一卒，卒偏之两。军行右辕，以辕为法，故挟辕而战，皆周制也。臣谓百人曰卒，五十人曰两，此是每车一乘，用士百五十人，此(比)周制差多尔。周一乘步卒七十二人，甲士三人。以二十五人为一甲，凡

【今译】

好准备。’这也是来源于周朝军制吗？”

李靖说：“按照《左传》记载，楚庄王的战车共有三十乘，每乘战车的士卒人数为一卒（100人），人数比周制每辆战车多一两（25人）。步卒在车的右边随车行动，以车辕为准，在两辆车之间进行战斗，这都是周代的制度。臣认为，按每百人为一卒，五十人为一两，这样每辆战车一乘，配用士卒一百五十人，比周代的编制人数增多了。周代一乘步卒七十二人，甲士三人。以二十五人为一甲，三甲共有

Guangs, King Zhuang of Chu said that 'officers at all levels should act in accordance with orders given with the flags and the troops should be ready without any instruction.' Did this also come out of the Zhou regulations?"

Li Jing said: "According to what is recorded in *Zuo Zhuan(Master Zuo's Commentary on the Spring and Autumn Annals)*, each '*Guang*' of the King Zhuang of Chu consisted of 30 chariots with one 'Zu' of troops (100 men). The number of the troops for each '*Guang*' was one more '*Liang*' (25 men) than that of Zhou. The foot soldiers advanced along with the chariots on their right, measured against the shafts and fighting between two chariots. These were all Zhou regulations. In my opinion, if each hundred troops comprised one 'Zu' and fifty troops comprised one 'Liang,' then there would be one hundred and fifty troops for each chariot, thus the number of troops was bigger than that of Zhou. In the case of Zhou, there were seventy-two troops and three armored officers for each chariot. If twenty-five men comprised one '*Jia*,' then three '*Jia*' would consist of seventy-five men. Chu State was a country of rivers

【原文】

三甲，共七十五人。楚山泽之国，车少而人多。分为三队，则与周制同矣。”

太宗曰：“春秋荀吴伐狄，毁车为行，亦正兵欤，奇兵欤？”

靖曰：“荀吴用车法尔，虽舍车而法在其中焉。一为左角，一为右角，一为前拒，分为三队，此一乘法也，千万乘皆然。臣按《曹公新书》云：攻车七十五人，前拒一队，左右角二队；守车一队，炊

【今译】

七十五人。楚国多山多水，车少人多，也将每辆战车的士卒分为三队，这种分队编制的基本方法是与周代制度相同的。”

唐太宗说：“春秋时晋国荀吴率军征伐狄国，舍弃车战改用步战。这是正兵还是奇兵？”

李靖说：“荀吴用的是车战的战法，虽然舍弃战车而改用步卒，但他的战法仍然是车战的。他以一队为左翼，一队为右翼，一队为中央前卫，共分三队，这是一乘战车的战斗队形，千乘万乘也是用照此类推的办法作前三角队形部署。我根据《曹公新书》的说法，战车一乘七十五人，中央前卫一队，

and mountains and had less chariots and more people. They also divided the troops for each chariot into three groups. This method of troop organization was the same as that of Zhou."

Tang Taizong said: "During the Spring and Autumn Period, when Xun Wu of Jin State led an expedition force against the state of Di, he abandoned the chariots and employed the foot soldiers. Is this an orthodox tactic or an unorthodox tactic?"

Li Jing said: "What Xun Wu conducted was a chariot warfare. Although he abandoned the chariots, his tactic was still one of chariot warfare. He set one group as the left flank, one as the right flank and one as the central vanguard, all these three groups formed the battle formation of one chariot. Whether one thousand or ten thousand chariots, such a delta-shaped deployment would be the same. According to the *New Book of Duke Cao*, there would be seventy-five troops for each assault chariot with one group as the central vanguard and one each as the left and right flanks; there would be one group for the logistic chariot with ten men to provide food, five to repair and maintain the equipment, five to

【原文】

子十人，守装五人，厩养五人，樵汲五人，共二十五人。攻守二乘，凡百人。兴兵十万，用车千乘，轻重二千，此大率荀吴之旧法也。又观汉魏之间军制：五车为队，仆射一人；十车为师，率长一人；凡车千乘，将吏二人。多多仿此。臣以今法参用之：则跳荡，骑兵也；战锋队，步骑相半也；驻队，兼车乘而出也。臣西讨突厥，越险数千里，此制未尝

【今译】

左右侧翼各一队；辎重、守备车一队，炊士人员十人，装备管理人员五人，饲养人员五人，砍柴挑水五人，共二十五人。攻守两车合计正好百人。这样兴兵十万，动用战车千乘，辎重守备车千乘，共要轻重战车二千乘，这就是荀吴当时车战编制的大概情况。再看汉魏时期的编制，五车为一队，设仆射一人，十车为一师，设率长一人。一千乘兵车，设将吏二人。依此类推，都是这样。臣现今编制部队的方法是以古法为参考的，就是：跳荡队，由骑兵编成；战锋队，由步、骑各半混合编成；驻队，由

care for the horses, five to gather firewood and fetch water —— altogether twenty-five men. The number of men for a pair of assault and logistic chariots totaled just one hundred. Thus if you send a force of one hundred thousand men, you would employ one thousand assault chariots and one thousand logistic chariots, totaling two thousand light and heavy chariots. This is the general organization of chariot warfare of Xun Wu at that time. Now let's have a look at the organization of the period from Han to Wei. At that time, five chariots composed a formation with one man as the commander; ten chariots formed a division with one man as the chief commandant. For each one thousand chariots, there would be two general officers. No matter how many chariots there were, the pattern would be the same. I have referred to the ancient methods when organizing our own forces: our probing force is composed of cavalry; the frontal assault force is made up of infantry and cavalry, half and half; the holding force is formed of foot soldiers and chariots. When I led the expedition force against the Turks in the west, we traveled thousands of li and overcame innumerable difficulties and ob-

【原文】

敢易。盖古法节制，信可重焉。"

太宗幸灵州回，召靖赐坐曰："朕命道宗及阿史那社尔等讨薛延陀，而铁勒诸部乞置汉官，朕皆从其请。延陀西走，恐为后患，故遣李勣讨之。今北荒悉平，然诸部番汉杂处，以何道经久，使得两全安之？"

靖曰："陛下敕自突厥至回纥部落，凡置驿六十六处，以通斥候，斯已得策矣。然臣愚以谓，汉戍宜自为一法，番落宜自为一法，教习各异，勿使

【今译】

步兵和战车编成。臣率军西讨突厥，越过艰难险阻数千里，这种编组方法也没敢轻易变动。古代军制严谨完整，确实应当重视啊。"

唐太宗巡幸灵州返回长安，召见李靖并赐坐，说："朕命令李道宗和阿史那社尔等率兵讨伐薛延陀，而铁勒各部落表示归顺，请求派置汉人官吏管辖。朕已答应他们的请求。薛延陀向西逃走，恐怕会成为后患，所以朕又派李勣率兵继续征讨。现在北方荒漠地区的外族基本都已平定，然而各部落的少数民族与汉族掺杂混合住在一块，你看用什么办法可以使少数民族与汉族长期共处相安无事？"

李靖说："陛下下令从突厥到回纥的所有部落共设置驿站六十六处，以利侦察兵往来传送情报，这已是很好的办法了。但愚臣以为，戍边的汉族部

stacles, even then I never dared to change this system. The ancient military regulations and organizations are truly well designed and complete and are really worth attention."

After an imperial tour of inspection to Ling Zhou, Tang Taizong returned to Chang'an. He summoned Li Jing, invited him to be seated and said: "I ordered Li Daozong, Ashinashe'er and others to lead a punitive expedition against Xue Yantuo. The Tie Le tribes have expressed their submission and requested to have some Han officials to govern them. I have acceded to their requests. Xue Yantuo fled to the west and would probably become a source of trouble to us, so I sent Li Ji to continue the expedition. Now the northern barbarous and remote areas are all settled and secured, but the minority peoples and the Han people now dwell intermingled with one another in all those tribes, what do you think we can do to make them live together for long and in peace?"

Li Jing said: "Your Majesty has ordered to set up sixty-six relay stations in all the tribes from Turk region to Uigur region to let the scouts to send information about the enemy.

【原文】

混同。或遇寇至，则密敕主将，临时变号易服，出奇击之。”

太宗曰：“何道也？”

靖曰：“此所谓‘多方以误之’之术也。番而示之汉，汉而示之番，彼不知番汉之别，则莫能测我攻守之计矣。善用兵者，先为不可测，则敌‘乖其所之’也。”

【今译】

队应当用一套训练管理办法，少数民族部队应当用另一套训练管理办法，分别进行训练，不能混合在一起。当遇到敌寇侵袭时，就密令主将，将汉族、少数民族的士卒临时变换旗号，改换装束，出其不意地打击敌人。”

太宗说：“这是什么道理呢？”

李靖说：“这就是古人所说‘多方以误之’（采取多种办法迷惑敌人、促使敌人犯错误）的方法。少数民族的士卒装做汉族士卒，汉族士卒装做少数民族的士卒，让敌人弄不明白番汉之别，就无法判断我方的攻守方略了。善于用兵的将领，先让敌人对我方企图无法判断，那么就能调动敌人、改变敌人行动的方向，也就是‘乖其所之’了。”

That is a measure already good enough. However, I think that the Han forces situated in the border areas should have a set of training methods and the minority another. They should be trained separately and should not be mixed up. When attacked by the enemy, you can secretly order the commanding general to change the flags and insignias of the Han and minority troops and have them exchange their uniforms so that they can take the enemy by surprise."

Tang Taizong said: "For what reason?"

Li Jing said: "This is the technique referred to by the ancients as 'using various ways to confuse the enemy and having him make mistakes.' If you have the minority troops appear as Han troops and Han troops as minority troops, the enemy will not know the distinction between the minority and Han and then will not be able to know our strategies of attacking and defending. A general good at battle commanding should first prevent the enemy from getting to know our intention, then he will be able to control the movement of the enemy and change the directions of their movement. This is called 'to divert the enemy from going where he wishes.'"

【原文】

太宗曰："正合朕意，卿可密教边将。只以此，番汉便见奇正之法矣。"

靖拜舞曰："圣虑天纵，闻一知十，臣安能极其说哉！"

太宗曰："诸葛亮言：'有制之兵，无能之将，不可败也；无制之兵，有能之将，不可胜也。'朕疑此谈非极致之论。"

靖曰："武侯有所激云尔。臣按《孙子》曰：'教道不明，吏卒无常，陈兵纵横，曰乱。'自古乱

【今译】

太宗说："这正符合朕的意图，你可用它秘密教授给戍边将领。只凭这套办法，番汉之兵的运用就可体现奇正变化的方法了。"

李靖拜伏行礼说："圣上的英明思考是上天赋予的，闻一知十，臣哪里能透彻地阐述其中的奥妙呢！"

唐太宗说："诸葛亮说过：'有制之兵，无能之将，不可败也；无制之兵，有能之将，不可胜也。'（有节制的军队，即使将领无能，也是不会打败仗的；没有节制的军队，即使将领有才能，也是没法打胜仗的）朕怀疑这话并非是精辟之论。"

李靖说："诸葛武侯的这番话是为了激励部队抓好训练加强素质而说的。臣按《孙子兵法》所说：'教道不明，吏卒无常，陈兵纵横，曰乱。'（将帅

Tang Taizong said: "That suits me fine. You can secretly teach it to our border generals. With this method, the change of the unorthodox and orthodox can be manifested through the employment of minority and Han troops."

Li Jing bowed and said: "The brilliant thoughts of Your Majesty are bestowed by Heaven. You learn one thing and understand ten. How could I be able to explain the secrecy of it so thoroughly as you do!"

Tang Taizong said: "Zhuge Liang said: 'A well-regulated army, even if commanded by an incompetent general, cannot be defeated; while a badly-regulated army, even if it has a capable general, will not win a victory.' I doubt that these remarks are insightful."

Li Jing said: "These remarks of Marquis Wu (Zhuge Liang) were made to encourage the troops to carry out strict training and to improve the troops' quality. I would quote what is said in *Sun Zi's Art of War* here: 'When the general is incompetent and has little authority, when his troops are mismanaged, when the relationship between officers and men is strained, and when the troop formations are slovenly, the result is

【原文】

军引胜，不可胜纪。夫教道不明者，言教阅无古法也；吏卒无常者，言将臣权任无久职也；乱军引胜者，言己自溃败，非敌胜之也。是以武侯言，兵卒有制，虽庸将未败；若兵卒自乱，虽贤将危之，又何疑焉？”

太宗曰：“教阅之法，信不可忽。”

靖曰：“教得其道，则士乐为用；教不得法，虽朝督暮责，无益于事矣。臣所以区区古制皆纂以

【今译】

懦弱又无威严，治军没有章法，官兵关系混乱紧张，布阵杂乱无章，必然自己搞乱自己，叫做‘乱’）自古以来由于己方军队混乱导致敌人取胜的战例数不胜数。所谓教道不明，说的是训练不遵照古法；所谓吏卒无常，说的是军官职务权力经常变动；所谓乱军引胜，说的是自己先溃败，并不是被敌人战胜的。所以诸葛武侯说：士卒训练有制，即使庸将带兵也不会打败仗；如果士卒不战自乱，即使是贤将带兵也是很危险的。这还有什么可怀疑的呢？”

太宗说：“教育训练的方法确实是不可忽视的。”

李靖说：“教育方法对头，则士卒会很高兴为我所用；教育不得法，即使对士卒早上督促、晚上责备也是无济于事的。臣之所以专心致志地钻研古

disorganization, then it is termed chaos.' Since antiquity, the cases where an army was defeated by the enemy due to its own chaos are too many to be counted. Here 'troops are mismanaged' is meant that the troops are not trained with the ancient methods; 'relationship between officers and men is strained' is meant that officers' posts are shifted too often; and 'defeated by the enemy due to 'its own chaos' is meant that the army was defeated by itself but not the enemy. That is why Marquis Wu said that if the troops are well-regulated, even if they are commanded by an incompetent general, they will not be defeated; if the troops themselves are in chaos before going into a battle, then even if they are led by a competent general, they will still be endangered. How can there be any doubt about it?"

Tang Taizong said: "The methods of education and training of troops truly can not be neglected."

Li Jing said: "Correct education methods will make the troops happy to be employed; if the methods are not correct, the training will come to nothing even if you supervise them in the morning and upbraid them in the evening. The

【原文】

图者，庶乎成有制之兵也。”

太宗曰：“卿为我择古阵法，悉图以上。”

太宗曰：“番兵唯劲马奔冲，此奇兵欤？汉兵唯强弩犄角，此正兵欤？”

靖曰：“按《孙子》云：‘善用兵者，求之于势，不贵(责)于人，故能择人而任势。’夫所谓择人者，各随番汉所长而战也。番长于马，马利乎速斗；汉长于弩，弩利乎缓战。此自然各任其势也，然非

【今译】

代兵法并把它们编纂成图，是希望把部队练成节制之师。”

太宗说：“请你为我选择古阵法，全部绘成图送上来。”

唐太宗说：“少数民族的军队倚仗骁勇战马奔突冲杀，这是奇兵吗？汉族军队倚仗强弓劲弩夹击敌人，这是正兵吗？”

李靖说：“《孙子兵法》说：‘善用兵者，求之于势，不责于人，故能择人而任势。’（善于用兵的将领，总是设法造成有利的态势，而不苛求部属，所以他能不强求人力去利用和创造有利的态势）所谓选择人手，就是让少数民族和汉族的士卒都能在战场上发挥自己的优长。少数民族的士兵长于骑射，

reason why I study ancient military regulations so carefully and collate them with diagrams is that I hope to train our army into a well-regulated one."

Tang Taizong said: "Please select the ancient methods for formations and diagram them all for me."

Tang Taizong said: "The minority armies rely on their strong war horses to rush forth to attack. Are they unorthodox forces? The Han armies rely on their strong crossbows to make pincer attacks on the enemy. Are they orthodox forces?"

Li Jing said: "According to *Sun Zi's Art of War:* 'A skilled commander sets great store by using the situation to the best advantage, and does not make excessive demand on his subordinates. Hence he is able to select right men and exploit the situation.' What is referred to as 'to select right men' means to let minority and Han troops give play to their respective advantages in the battlefield. Minority soldiers excel in fighting on the horses and have an advantage in battles of quick decision; Han soldiers excel in

【原文】

奇正所分。臣前曾部(述)番汉必变号易服者，奇正相生之法也。马亦有正，弩亦有奇，何常之有哉!”

太宗曰：“卿更细言其术。”

靖曰：“先形之，使敌从之，是其术也。”

太宗曰：“朕悟之矣！《孙子》曰：‘形兵之极，至于无形’，又曰：‘因形而措胜于众，众不能知。’其此之谓乎?”

靖再拜曰：“深乎！陛下圣虑，已思过半矣。”

【今译】

骑马利于速决战；汉族士兵长于弓弩，弓弩适合缓战。这都是顺其自然地发挥他们各自的优势，但不是奇正的区分。臣以前曾经讲述番汉士卒变换旗号装束的办法，那正是奇正相生的办法。马战有正有奇，弩战也是有奇有正，哪里有固定不变的道理!”

太宗说：“爱卿再详细解释一下。”

李靖说：“先给敌人制造一些假象，使敌人听从我的调动，就是这种办法。”

太宗说：“朕领悟了！《孙子》说：‘形兵之极，至于无形’（伪装佯动做到最好的地步，就看不出形迹），又说：‘因形而措胜于众，众不能知。’(根据敌情变化而灵活运用战术，即使把胜利摆在众人面前，众人还是看不出其中奥妙）说的是这种情况吧?”

李靖再拜说：“这是兵法中多么深奥的道理啊!

crossbows and have an advantage in slow-paced battles. In this, they naturally give play to what they are good at but should not be considered as a distinction of unorthodox and orthodox. Previously, I discussed how to let minority and Han troops change their flags and exchange their uniforms, that is how unorthodox and orthodox mutually transform into each other. There are orthodox and unorthodox in horse warfare and there are unorthodox and orthodox in crossbow warfare. Nowhere is there any hard and fast rule!"

Tang Taizong said: "Please explain it in detail."

Li Jing said: "First to create a false impression and then have the enemy move at our will, that is the technique."

Tang Taizong said: "I understand it now. Sun Zi said in his *Art of War:* 'The ultimate in disposing the troops is to conceal them without ascertainable shape.' He also said: 'Even though we show people the victory gained by using flexible tactics in conformity to the changing situations, they do no comprehend this.' Is this what it means?"

Li Jing bowed again and said: "How abstruse

【原文】

太宗曰："近契丹、奚皆内属，置松漠、饶乐二都督，统于安北都护。朕用薛万彻，如何？"

靖曰："万彻不如阿史那社尔及执失思力、契妍(苾)何力，此皆番臣之知兵者也。因常与之言松漠、饶乐山川道路，番情逆顺，远至于西域部落十数种，历历可信。臣教之以阵法，无不点头服义。望陛下任之勿疑。若万彻，则勇而无谋，难以独任。"

【今译】

陛下天资聪颖，现在就已领悟过半了。"

太宗说："最近契丹人、奚人都来归顺，朝廷设置了松漠、饶乐两处都督府，统归安北都护府管辖。朕考虑起用薛万彻，你觉得怎样？"

李靖说："薛万彻的才能不如阿史那社尔和执失思力、契苾何力等人。这几位是少数民族官员中谙熟兵法的人。我曾经和他们谈论过松漠、饶乐的山川形势、道路状况，以及少数民族部落对我朝的顺逆情况。甚至远到西域的十多个部落的情况，他们都谈得一清二楚，令人信服。我教授他们阵法，他们无不点头佩服。希望陛下任用他们，不必怀疑。至于薛万彻，有勇无谋，难以独当重任。"

are these ideas of the art of war! Your Majesty is bright and talented and has comprehended already more than half of it."

Tang Taizong said: "Recently, the Khitan and Xi peoples have all submitted. The two Commanders-in-Chief appointed by the imperial court at Song Mo and Rao Le will be jointly put under the administration of the Supreme Commander at An Bei. I would like to give the post to Xue Wanche. How do you think?"

Li Jing said: "Xue Wanche is not so capable as Ashinashe'er, Zhishisili and Qibiheli. They are the few among the minority officials who understand military affairs. I once discussed with them about the mountains, rivers and roads of Song Mo and Rao Le as well as the submissive and rebellious minorities. The information they gave of all these is very detailed and convincing; they even talked about the dozen tribes as far out as in the western region. I taught them formation manoeuvers and in each case they would nod their admiration. I hope that Your Majesty will entrust and employ them without having any doubt. As for Xue Wanche, he is courageous but not resourceful, and it will be very difficult for

【原文】

太宗笑曰：“番人皆为卿役使！古人云，以蛮夷攻蛮夷，中国之势也。卿得之矣。”

【今译】

太宗笑着说：“少数民族人都为你所用了！古人说，以蛮夷治蛮夷，中国历来的情势大体如此。你已经懂得这个道理。”

him to bear the responsibility alone."

Tang Taizong smiled and said: "These minority people have all been used by you! The ancients said: 'To use the barbarians to govern the barbarians, that is the general way of government for the Central State.' Now you have understood it."

卷中

【原文】

太宗曰："朕观诸兵书，无出孙武。孙武十三篇，无出《虚实》。夫用兵，识虚实之势，则无不胜焉。今诸将中，但能言背实击虚，及其临敌，则鲜识虚实者，盖不能致人，而反为敌所致故也。如何？卿悉为诸将言其要。"

靖曰："先教之以奇正相变之术，然后语之以

【今译】

唐太宗说："朕读过各种兵书，没有超过孙武所著《孙子兵法》的。孙武的十三篇兵法中，没有超出《虚实》一篇的。用兵作战，只要懂得敌我虚实形势，没有不打胜仗的。现在的将领中，只是在口头上会说避实击虚，等到真的和敌人交战，就很少有人能看清战场的虚实情势了，不能够调动敌人，而反为敌人所调动。你认为怎么样？你可以全面地给将领们讲解有关虚实的要领。"

李靖说："先教会他们奇正相互变化的方法，然后再告诉他们识别虚实的各种情形，这样就容易

BOOK II

Tang Taizong said: "I have gone through all the military books, but none of them surpasses *Sun Zi's Art of War* written by Sun Wu, and of the thirteen chapters of this book, none surpasses the chapter of 'Weaknesses and Strengths.' When fighting a war, if you are aware of the weaknesses and strengths both of the enemy's and your own, you will always be victorious. Most of the contemporary generals are only able to talk about steering clear of the enemy's main strength and attacking where he is weak, but when they are engaging the enemy, few of them are able to discern the weaknesses and strengths in the battlefield. They are unable to have the enemy move but are themselves moved by the enemy. How do you think about this? You may discuss the essentials of all these in detail with our generals."

Li Jing said: "First to teach them the techniques for mutual change of the unorthodox and

【原文】

虚实之形可也。诸将多不知以奇为正，以正为奇，且安识虚是实，实是虚哉?"

太宗曰："'策之而知得失之计，作之而知动静之理，形之而知死生之地，角之而知有余不足之处。'此则奇正在我，虚实在敌欤?"

靖曰："奇正者，所以致敌之虚实也。敌实，则我必以正；敌虚，则我必为奇。苟将不知奇正，

【今译】

领悟了。将领们大都不知道把奇兵变为正兵、把正兵变为奇兵，那怎么能识破敌人的虚是实、实是虚呢?"

太宗说："孙武所说'策之而知得失之计，作之而知动静之理，形之而知死生之地，角之而知有余不足之处。'（筹算一下计谋，来分析敌人作战计划的优劣；挑动一下敌军，来了解敌人的活动规律；侦察一下情况，来了解哪里有利哪里不利；进行一下小战，来了解敌人兵力虚实强弱）这不是说奇正变化在我这方、是虚是实在敌一方吗?"

李靖说："变化奇正，是为了察明和对付敌人的虚实。敌人兵阵坚实，那我就用正兵对付它；敌人兵力虚弱，那我就用奇兵对付它。假若将领不知

orthodox and tell them about how to discern weaknesses and strengths in different situations, thus it will be easy for them to understand. Most of the generals do not know how to use unorthodox forces as orthodox ones and orthodox as unorthodox, then how can they recognize when the weak is actually strong while the strong is actually weak?"

Tang Taizong said: "Sun Wu said: 'Analyze the enemy's battle plan, so as to have a clear understanding of its strong and weak points. Agitate the enemy, so as to ascertain his pattern of movement. Lure him in the open so as to find out his vulnerable spots in disposition. Probe him and learn where his strength is abundant and where deficient.' Isn't this meant that the change of unorthodox and orthodox lies with us while whether it is weak or strong lies with the enemy?"

Li Jing said: "To change unorthodox and orthodox into each other is to find out and cope with enemy's weaknesses and strengths. If the enemy's formation is solid and strong, I will use orthodox forces to deal with it; if the enemy forces are weak, then I will use unorthodox

【原文】

则虽知敌虚实，安能致之哉？臣奉诏，但教诸将以奇正，然后虚实自知焉。”

太宗曰：“以奇为正者，敌意其奇，则吾正击之；以正为奇者，敌意其正，则吾奇击之。使敌势常虚，我势常实。当以此法授诸将，使易晓尔。”

靖曰：“千章万句，不出乎‘致人而不致于人’

【今译】

道奇正变化，即使知道了敌人虚实，又怎么能调动他们呢？我遵照您的旨意，只要教会将领们奇正的运用，他们自然就会懂得识别虚实的道理了。”

太宗说：“把奇兵当成正兵使用，敌人仍当它是奇兵来对待，则我以正兵打击敌人；把正兵变为奇兵使用，敌人仍当它是正兵，则我以奇兵打击敌人。这样可使敌人的态势总是虚弱，我方态势总是坚实。应当把这种方法传授给将领，使他们容易明白。”

李靖说：“兵法千章万句，阐述的道理都不外乎‘致人而不致于人’（调动敌人而不被敌人所调

forces to fight with them. If a general does not know the change of unorthodox and orthodox, even if he knows where the enemy is weak and where is strong, how can he be able to bring him in? I will respectfully abide by your decree. If the generals are taught to know how to employ the unorthodox and orthodox, then they will know how to recognize the weak and the strong."

Tang Taizong said: "If we use the unorthodox as the orthodox and the enemy still takes it as unorthodox, then we will use the orthodox to attack the enemy; if we use the orthodox as the unorthodox, and the enemy still takes it as orthodox, then we will use the unorthodox to attack him. Thus the enemy will be kept always vulnerable and we stay strong. You should teach the generals these methods so as to have them understand it more easily."

Li Jing said: "There are thousands of articles and tens of thousands of words about military strategy and tactics, but none of them will go beyond the principle of 'bringing the enemy to battle and not being brought there by him.' I will certainly use this fundamental principle to

【原文】

而已。臣当以此教诸将。”

太宗曰：“朕置瑶池都督，以隶安西都护。番汉之兵，如何处置？”

靖曰：“天之生人，本无番汉之别。然地远荒漠，必以射猎而生，由此常习战斗。若我恩信抚之，衣食周之，则皆汉人矣。陛下置此都护，臣请收汉戍卒，处之内地，减省粮馈，兵家所谓治力之法也。

【今译】

动）罢了。臣一定用这条根本道理去教育将领。”

唐太宗说：“朕设置瑶池都督，隶属于安西都护府管辖。这是少数民族和汉族士兵杂处的地方，应该怎样治理呢？”

李靖说：“人刚生下来的时候，本来不存在番汉差别。但是因为地处偏远荒漠，少数民族人必须以猎狩为生，因而也就经常地练习战斗。如果我们施恩示信抚慰他们，在衣着食物上周济他们，则都和汉人一样臣服于我了。陛下设置这个都护府，臣请能撤出汉兵戍卒，移防内地，减省粮秣，这就是兵家所说‘治力’的方法啊。只要挑选熟悉少数民

teach the generals."

Tang Taizong said: "I have appointed a Commander-in-Chief at Yao Chi subordinate to the Office of An Xi Supreme Commander. This is an area where the minority people and Han troops live together, how shall we manage and govern the area?"

Li Jing said: "People are not born barbarian or Han. But the minority peoples live in the remote barbarous desert and have to live on hunting. That is why they constantly practice fighting. If we are generous to them, show good faith to them, console them and supply them with clothes and food, then they will submit to us like the Han people. As Your Majesty has established the Office of An Xi Supreme Commander,please allow me to request you to withdraw the border Han troops to the interior and reduce the provisions. This is what the strategists refer to as the art of 'husbanding the strength.' You can select some Han officials who are familiar with the affairs of the minority areas and allocate them to the defense of the border cities and fortifications, and this will be sufficient to manage these areas for a long time. If we en-

【原文】

但择汉吏有熟番情者，散守堡障，此足以经久。或遇有警，则虞(汉)卒出焉。”

太宗曰：“《孙子》所言治力何如?”

靖曰：“‘以近待远，以佚待劳，以饱待饥’，此略言其概尔。善用兵者，推此三义而有六焉：以诱待来，以静待躁，以重待轻，以严待懈，以治待乱，以守待攻。反是，则力有弗逮。非治之(力)之术，安能临兵哉!”

太宗曰：“今人习《孙子》者，但诵空文，鲜

【今译】

族地区情况的汉人官吏，分别防守边城寨堡，这样足以长久治理。遇到有警的时候，汉兵可立即出动。”

太宗说：“《孙子兵法》里说的‘治力’是怎么回事?”

李靖说：“‘以近待远，以佚待劳，以饱待饥’(用自己部队的接近战场对付远道而来的敌人，用自己部队的安逸休整对付奔走疲劳的敌人，用自己部队的饱食对付饥饿的敌人)，这只是大概地说了一下‘治力’。善于用兵的人，可以把这三条原理推论到六种情形：以诱惑等待敌人落入圈套，以冷静等待敌人急躁冒进，以持重等待敌人轻举妄动，以严整等待敌人懈怠松弛，以整治等待敌人内部混乱，以固守等待敌人发动进攻。与之相反，战斗力就不能保持。不懂得保持战斗力的方法，怎么能带兵打仗!”

太宗说：“现在学习《孙子兵法》的人，只知道背诵条文，很少有能引申发挥‘治力’之法的。

counter some emergency, the Han troops can go out there immediately."

Tang Taizong said: "What is then the 'husbanding the strength' in *Sun Zi's Art of War*?"

Li Jing said: " 'Await an enemy coming from afar with our troops close to the field of battle; await an exhausted enemy with our troops at rest; await a hungry enemy with our troops well-fed.' This only gives a rough explanation of the 'husbanding the strength.' Those who are good at battle tactics can develop these three principles into six: 'With enticement await the enemy's falling into traps. In quiescence await the enemys' impetuous advance. With prudence await the enemy's impulsive move. With readiness await the enemy's slackness. With order await the enemy's disorder. With solid defense await the enemy's attack. Vice versa, you will lose your capability. How can one lead his men into a battle if he does not know how to keep his capability?"

Tang Taizong said: "People who study *Sun Zi's Art of War* today only know to recite the words, few of them know how to develop and

【原文】

克推广其义。治力之法，宜遍告诸将。”

太宗曰：“旧将老卒，凋零殆尽，诸军新置，不经阵敌。今教以何道为要？”

靖曰：“臣尝教士，分为三等：必先结伍法，伍法既成，授之军校，此一等也；军校之法，以一为十，以十为百，此一等也；授之裨将，裨将乃总诸校之队，聚为阵图，此一等也。大将军察此三等

【今译】

应该普遍地告诉每一个将领。”

唐太宗说：“旧将老兵，剩下的已经不多了，各部队都是新组建的，没有经历过实战。现在对他们进行训练应该采用什么方法才是最重要的？”

李靖说：“我以往训练部队，分为三个阶段：首先是五人一伍，进行伍法训练，伍法训练好后，交由军校训练，这是一个阶段。军校训练的方法是一伍学成之后将十伍编成一队进行训练，十伍学成之后再将百伍编成一队进行训练，这是又一个阶段。此后再将部队交给副将训练，副将把各军校训练过的部队合起来，按一定的阵法、阵形进行训练，这是第三阶段。大将军视察这三个阶段训练的成效，

give play to the art of 'husbanding the strength.' This should be expounded to all the generals."

Tang Taizong said: "We have not many old officers and soldiers left. Most of them are dead. The armies are newly organized and do not have any experience in combat. What are the essential training methods we shall apply for them?"

Li Jing said: "Previously, I used to train the troops in three steps: First, form squads of five men and train them with the method of squad training. After the squad training is completed, the training will be passed into the hands of the field officer. This is one step. The training by the field officer is that, after the squad training, he would first start the platoon training consisting of ten squads, and then the battalion training consisting of one hundred squads after the platoon training is completed. This is another step. After that, the troops will be in the hands of the assistant general who would organize all the troops trained by the field officers into an army and train them in accordance with certain methods and dispositions of formation. This is the third step. The commanding general will examine the results of the training of the three steps.

【原文】

之教，于是大阅，稽考制度，分别奇正，誓众行罚。陛下临高观之，无施不可。”

太宗曰：“伍法有数家，孰者为要？”

靖曰：“臣按《春秋左氏传》云，先偏后伍；又《司马法》曰，五人为伍；《尉缭子》有束伍令；汉制有尺籍伍符。后世符籍，以纸为之，于是失其制矣。臣酌其法，自五人而变为二十五人。自二十

【今译】

于是进行大阅，检查并考核制度落实情况，区别奇兵和正兵的划分和使用，告诫全军将士，惩处违犯军令者。此时陛下登临高台视察部队演练，整个军阵无论怎样指挥调动都能令行禁止、气势严整。”

太宗说：“训练伍法的方法有好几家，哪一家是主要的？”

李靖说：“据我所知，《春秋左氏传》里说：战车在前，步卒在后，步卒在战车队形的间隔与战车协同作战；《司马法》里说：五人组成一伍，作为战术、训练单位；《尉缭子》里有记载约束部伍的条令；汉朝的军事制度中有关于尺籍和伍符的规定。以后的军队符籍都是用纸做的，于是失去了这种古制的原貌。我参照这些古法，采取由五人变为

He will review the whole organization,check the assessment system, distinguish the troops into unorthodox and orthodox forces, and give warnings and punish those who disobey commands and orders. Then Your Majesty will come to inspect the exercise of the troops on a high platform and see that the formations operate exactly at the commands and orders and the whole army is full of power and grandeur."

Tang Taizong said: "There are several schools of thought on the methods for squad training, which of them is the most important?"

Li Jing said: "As to my knowledge, it is recorded in the *Master Zuo's Commentary on the Spring and Autumn* Annals that 'the chariots are in the front with the foot soldiers behind, the foot soldiers will fight accompanying the chariots between the chariot formations.' *The Methods of the "Sima"* states that 'five men make up a squad of five as the tactical training unit.' The *Wei Liao Zi* has a section entitled 'Regulations for Binding the Squads.' In the Han Dynasty, the military had the system of Bamboo Strip for

【原文】

五人而变为七十五人。此则步卒七十二人，甲士三人之制也。舍车用骑，则二十五人当八马，此则五兵五当之制也。是则诸家兵法，唯伍法为要。小列之五人，大列之二十五人，参列之七十五人。又五参其数，得三百七十五人。三百人为正，六十人为奇。此则百五十人分为二正，而三十人分为二奇，

【今译】

二十五人的做法，再由二十五人变为七十五人。这是仿照古制中一乘战车有步卒七十二人、甲士三人的编制。不用战车而使用骑兵作战时，以八马为一伍，相当于步卒二十五人。这就是根据‘五兵五当’原则运用车、步、骑的方法。由此可见诸家兵法都突出了伍法训练的重要性。最小的战术编组单位是五人，最大的战术编组单位是二十五人，由三个最大单位组成一个战术群为七十五人，那么五个战术群就是三百七十五人。以三百人用作正兵，以六十人用作奇兵。这样左右各以一百五十人分为二正、

Merit and Insignia for Squad. Later on, these strips and insignias began to be made out of paper, and thus losing their original looks as in the ancient times. I made reference with these ancient methods and adopted a method by changing the squad of five into a squad of twenty-five and then from twenty-five into seventy-five. This imitates the ancient organization of one chariot with seventy-two foot soldiers and three armored officers. When using cavalry instead of chariots, eight horses will form a squad which is equivalent to the infantry squad of twenty-five. This is the way to employ chariot, infantry and cavalry according to the principle of 'five men squad or the equivalent.' From this, we can see that all schools think very high of the training of the squad of five. The smallest tactical unit is composed of five men, the largest unit is of twenty-five, three largest units form a tactical group of seventy-five, then five tactical groups will consist of three hundred and seventy-five men, of which three hundred will be used as the orthodox force and sixty as the unorthodox. Thus there will be one orthodox force of one hundred and fifty troops and one unorthodox

【原文】

盖左右等也。穰苴所谓五人为伍，十伍为队，至今因之，此其要也。”

太宗曰：“朕与李勣论兵，多同卿说，但勣不究出处尔。卿所制六花阵法，出何术乎？”

靖曰：“臣所本诸葛亮八阵法也。大阵包小阵，大营包小营，隅落钩连，曲折相对。古制如此，臣为图因之。故外画之方，内环之圆，是成六花，俗所号尔？”

太宗曰：“内圆外方，何谓也？”

靖曰：“方生于正，圆生于奇。方所以矩其步，

【今译】

三十人分为二奇，左右相等。司马穰苴所讲五人为伍，十伍为队，是基本的军队编组方法，沿用至今。这些就是伍法的大体情况。”

唐太宗说：“朕与李勣谈论兵书，他的见解大体和你相同，但李勣不考究出处。你所创制的‘六花’阵法根据的是什么？”

李靖说：“我所依据的是诸葛亮的八阵法。大阵之中包含小阵，大营之内包含小营，四方四隅相互衔接，一曲一折彼此对应，古代阵法就是这个样子。我创制的阵法承袭这种原则，因此我的阵法外面六阵绘成方形，中军阵形绘成圆形，因此成了六角花瓣状，如同俗称的那样。”

太宗说：“内圆外方，这是为什么？”

李靖说：“外面六阵是实地的正兵，所以绘成方形；中央军阵处在机动位置，是阵中奇兵，所以

force of thirty each on both flanks equally. What Sima Rangju said about five men as a squad and ten squads as a platoon is the basic method of organizing the troops and it has been in use to this day. This is the method of the squad of five in general."

Tang Taizong said: "I discussed military books with Li Ji. His understanding of them for the most part accords with yours. But he does not examine the sources. What is your 'Six Pedals Formation' based upon?"

Li Jing said: "It is based on Zhuge Liaug's Eight Formations. Large formations contain small formations; large encampments contain small encampments. The four sides and four corners are interlocked and zigzagged in an equal way. The ancient formation was just like this and I copied it. So the outside of my formation is drawn to be square but the inside central formation is circular. Thus it gives the shape of a hexagon like a flower's six pedals, just as commonly termed."

Tang Taizong said: "Why is outside square and inside circular?"

Li Jing said: "The outside six formations are

【原文】

圆所以缀其旋。是以步数定于地，行缀应于天。步定缀齐，则变化不乱。八阵为六，武侯之旧法焉。”

太宗曰：“画方以见步，点圆以见兵，步教足法，兵教手法，手足便利，思过半矣。”

【今译】

绘成圆形。方阵是为了规定行进步数以使队形整齐划一；圆阵是为了随时可向各个方向出击和增援。因此方阵间隔的步数就像大地一样固定，圆阵回旋的线路就要像天体运动一样灵活。步数固定，回旋整齐，便可实现队形无论怎么变化都不会混乱。从八阵演变为六花阵，用的仍是诸葛亮的布阵原理。”

太宗说：“外画方形以显示步法，内画圆形以显示兵器。步幅要能行进准确，必须加强足法训练；兵器要能使用灵活，必须练习手上功夫。奇兵操作使用武器的功夫和正兵进退节奏步伐都训练好了，那就可以说对古人用兵布阵的道理掌握一大半了。”

李靖说：“吴起曾这样论述：‘绝而不离，却而不散’（虽然整个阵形被隔断，但每个小阵仍保持各自的阵形；虽然阵形被冲散，但仍能恢复行

orthodox troops to hold the positions, so the outside is drawn to be square; the central formation is the manoeuver force thus the unorthodox, so the inside is drawn to be circular. The square provides the means to regulate the paces and keep the formation integrated; the circle gives chances to attack and reinforce in any direction at any time. The number of the paces is as fixed as the Earth and the circulation of the cycle is as flexible as movement in Heaven. If the number of the paces is fixed and the circulation is in order, the changes of the formation will never be in disorder. Although the Eight Formations has been developed into the Six Pedals Formation, the method I use is still that of Zhuge Liang's."

Tang Taizong said: "To draw the square outside is to indicate the paces; to draw the cycle inside is to indicate the weapons. To keep the paces straight, one must have more practice on 'foot' techniques; to be good at weapons, one must practice hand techniques. If the unorthodox troops are trained to be good at their weapons and the orthodox troops good at paces, then we can say that more than half of the ancient methods of formation deployment have been

【原文】

靖曰："吴起云：'绝而不离，却而不散'，此步法也。教士犹布棋于盘，若无画路，棋安用之？孙武曰：'地生度，度生量，量生数，数生称，称生胜。胜兵若以镒称铢，败兵若以铢称镒'，皆起于度量方国(圆)也。"

太宗曰："深乎，孙武之言！不度地之远近，形之广狭，则何以制其节乎？"

靖曰："庸将罕能知其节者也。'善战者，其

【今译】

列)，这是步法训练的结果。教育士兵如同在棋盘上摆棋子一样，如果没画好棋路，棋子怎么能用呢？孙武说：'地生度，度生量，量生数，数生称，称生胜。胜兵若以镒称铢，败兵若以铢称镒'（敌我所处地域的不同，产生双方土地面积大小不同的'度'；敌我土地面积大小的'度'的不同，产生双方物资资源多少不同的'量'；敌我物产资源多少的'量'的不同，产生双方兵员多寡不同的'数'；敌我兵员多寡的'数'的不同，产生双方军事实力强弱不同的'称'；敌我军事实力强弱的'称'的不同，最终决定战争的胜负成败。胜利的军队较之于失败的军队，有如以'镒'称'铢'那样占有绝对的优势；失败的军队较之于胜利的军队，就像用'铢'称'镒'那样处于绝对的劣势），这都是从分析一国幅员大小、地形等情况开始的。"

太宗说："孙武的论述太深刻了！不考虑作战地域的远近、不考虑战场地形的广狭，怎么能控制好部队进退、攻守的节奏呢？"

李靖说："庸将很少能懂得进退攻守的节奏的。

mastered."

Li Jing said: "Wu Zi stated: 'Although the whole formation is separated, each small phalanx will still hold its own; although the formation can be torn apart, the arrays will still be kept intact.' This comes from the training of paces. To instruct the troops is just like placing chessmen on a chessboard. If there are no lines on the board, how can the chessmen be placed? Sun Wu said: 'Measurements of space are derived from the ground. Quantities derive from the measurement, figures from quantities, comparisons from figures and victory from comparisons. Therefore, a victorious army is as a hundredweight balanced against a grain, and a defeated army is as a grain balanced against a hundredweight.' It all commences with measuring the size and terrain of a state."

Tang Taizong said: "How profound are Sun Wu's remarks! If one does not consider the distance and size of the battle area, how can he have a good control of the tempo of his troops' advancing and retreating and attacking and defending?"

Li Jing said: "An incompetent general is

【原文】

势险，其节短，势加(如)彍弩，节如发机。’臣修其术：凡立队，相去各十步；驻队去前队二十步；每隔一队立一战队。前进以五十步为节。角一声，诸队皆散立，不过十步之内。至第四角声，笼枪跪坐。于是鼓之，三呼三击，三十步至五十步以制敌之变。马军从背出，亦五十步临时节止。前正后奇，观敌如何。再鼓之，则前奇后正，复邀敌来，伺隙捣虚。此

【今译】

《孙子兵法》说：‘善战者，其势险，其节短，势如彍弩，节如发机。’（善于指挥作战的人，他所造成的态势是险峻的，行动的节奏是短促的。险峻的态势就像张满的弯弓，短促的节奏就像击发弩机）我研究了这样的战术：凡是立队，每队之间距离十步，驻队距离前队二十步，每隔一队立一战锋队。每次前进，以五十步为一节。第一次角声响过，各队就地立正，彼此距离不超过十步。到第四角声响过，各队都要成荷枪跪坐姿势。于是击鼓前进，各队呼喊三次，击刺三次，前进到距敌人三十步至五十步的位置，以压制敌人使他们无法采取应变措施。与此同时，马军从阵后向前机动，也是以五十步为一节。前阵布列正兵，后阵布列奇兵，以观察敌人动静。再一次击鼓，前阵变为奇兵，后阵变为正兵，

rarely able to know that tempo. *Sun Zi's Art of War* states: 'A good commander creates a posture releasing an irresistible and overwhelming momentum, and his attacks are precisely timed in a quick tempo. The energy is similar to a fully drawn crossbow, and the timing is just like the release of the trigger.' I have worked out such a tactic: The standing platoons are ten paces apart from each other, the holding platoons are twenty paces from the platoons before them; for every other platoon will be emplaced a combat platoon. When advancing, fifty paces is one measure. After the first blowing of the horn, all platoons will stand still with the distance between each other not exceeding ten paces. After the fourth blowing of the horn, each platoon will position their spears and squat down. Then they will advance with the drums beaten, each platoon shouting three times and striking three times until they are thirty to fifty paces away from the enemy so as to prevent the enemy from taking any responding actions. At this time, the cavalry will move forward from the rear, also advancing fifty paces at a time. The front is orthodox and the rear unorthodox while observing

【原文】

六花大率皆然也。”

太宗曰：“《曹公新书》云：‘作阵对敌，必先立表，引兵就表而阵。一部受敌，余部不进救者斩。’此何术乎？”

靖曰：“临敌立表，非也。此但教战时法尔。古人善用兵者，教正不教奇，驱众若驱群羊，与之进，与之退，不知所之也。曹公骄而好胜，当时诸将奉《新书》者，莫敢攻其短。且临敌立表，无乃晚乎？臣窃观陛下所制破阵乐舞，前出四表，后缀

【今译】

再次向敌人挑战，乘敌之隙击其虚弱。六花阵法的战术大概如此。”

唐太宗说：“《曹公新书》中说：‘作阵对敌，必先立表，引兵就表而阵。一部受敌，余部不进救者斩。’（布阵对敌，必须先设立一标帜，然后率领部队按标帜布阵。当某一部分遭敌攻击时，其余部队不向前救援的要斩首）这是什么战术？”

李靖说：“到了和敌人交战时才设立标帜的说法是不正确的，这只不过是平时训练部队才用的方法。古时候善于用兵的人，只教练正兵的战法而不教练奇兵的战法，指挥士兵如同驱赶羊群，叫他们进就进，叫他们退就退，他们不知道自己要去哪里。曹操骄傲而又好胜，当时奉行《新书》的将领没有

the enemy's response. Then beat the drums and challenge the enemy again with the front as unorthodox and the rear orthodox, watching for an opening and attacking his weak points. The 'Six Pedals Formation' is generally like this."

Tang Taizong said: "The *New Book of Duke Cao* says: 'When you deploy your formation opposite the enemy, you must first set up a pennant and bring your troops into formation in line with that pennant. When one part is attacked by the enemy, any other part that does not come to its rescue will be beheaded.' What tactic is this?"

Li Jing said: "It is not correct to set up a pennant when engaging the enemy. This is a method only for training in peace time. The ancient good commanders merely taught orthodox tactics but not unorthodox tactics. They drove the troops like driving a herd of sheep. Advancing or retreating, they did not know where they were going. Cao Cao was arrogant and eager to excel in everything. No general who followed the *New Book* at his time dared to rake up his shortcomings. Moreover, if you set up a pennant when the enemy has already been engaged, isn't it too late? I have watched the musical dance

【原文】

八幡，左右折旋，趋步金鼓，各有其节，此即八阵图四头八尾之制也。人间但见乐舞之盛，岂有知军容如斯焉！”

太宗曰：“昔汉高帝定天下，歌云：‘安得猛士兮，守四方！’盖兵法可以意授，不可以语传。朕为破阵乐舞，唯卿已晓其表矣，后世其知我不苟作也。”

太宗曰：“方色五旗为正乎？幡麾折冲为奇乎？

【今译】

人敢揭露其短处。更何况同敌人交战时才设立标帜，不是太晚了吗？我看陛下创制的‘破阵乐舞’，先出示四面标帜，然后排列八幅长幡，舞蹈者或左或右进退回旋，那步法随着金鼓之声或快或慢，各有节奏，这就是八阵图中四头八尾的精神。人们只是看到了音乐舞蹈的盛况，哪里知道这里包含深奥的阵法道理呢！”

太宗说：“当年汉高祖刘邦平定天下以后曾唱道：‘安得猛士兮，守四方！’（怎能得到勇士啊，守卫四方）兵法可以意会，但不可以言传。朕创制‘破阵乐舞’，唯有你已领悟它所表达的深意，后来的人大概可以知道我不是随随便便创作的了。”

唐太宗说：“在东、南、西、北、中五个方位上分别使用青、赤、白、黑、黄五种颜色的旗帜布

'Destroying the Formation' created by Your Majesty.First come four pennants and then eight long narrow flags are deployed. Left or right, back or forth, the dancers are dancing and whirling with their paces quite to the tempo of the sound of drums. This is the spirit of the four heads and eight tails in the Eight Formations Diagram. People only see the flourishing of the dance but do not know that the dance contains the secrecy of the deployment art."

Tang Taizong said: "In antiquity, when the Emperor of the Han Dynasty Liu Bang settled the realm, he once sang: 'Where can I get fierce warriors to guard the four quarters?' Military strategies can be sensed but cannot be explained in words. I created the musical dance of 'Destroying the Formation,' only you understand what it implies. So, people in later generations will know that I created it not in a careless way."

Tang Taizong said: "When flags in five colors—green, red, white, black and yellow—are used in five directions—to the east, south, west, north and in the center—to deploy the formation, is it orthodox? When various streamers and pennants are employed to command the troops,

【原文】

分合为变，其队数曷为得宜?”

靖曰：“臣参用古法：凡三队合，则旗相倚而不变；五队合，则两旗交；十队合，则五旗交。吹角，开五交之旗，则一复散而为十；开二交之旗，则一复散而为五；开相倚不交之旗，则一复散而为三。兵散，则以合为奇；合，则以散为奇。三令五申，三散(三)合，然复归于正，四头八尾乃可教焉。此队法所宜也。”

【今译】

阵，这是正兵吗？用各种长幡、小旗灵活指挥部队，这是奇兵吗？队形的分散和集中变化过程中，其队数为多少才算适宜？”

李靖说：“我参照古人的办法，凡是三队合为一队，旗帜只是并列而不交叉；当五队合为一队时，则两旗交叉；十队合为一队，用五旗交叉。吹起角声，分开五面交叉的旗子，则十队合成的一队又分成十队；分开两面交叉的旗子，则五队合成的一队又分成五队；只是并列而不交叉的旗子分开，则三队合成的一队又分成三队。部队分散时就以集中为奇；部队集中时就以分散为奇。经过三令五申，反复练习分散和集中，然后再归于正兵的训练。这样就可以按四头八尾的阵法进行正式教练了。这是训练阵法比较适宜的办法。”

is it unorthodox? The formation changes in splitting and assembling, in the process, how many platoons are needed there to be appropriate?"

Li Jing said: "I have employed the ancient method: when three platoons combine, the flags go parallel and are not crossed; when five platoons combine, two flags are crossed; when ten platoons combine, five flags are crossed. With the blow of the horn, the five crossed flags are separated and the formation combined by ten will split again into ten platoons; when the two crossed flags are separated, the formation combined by five will split again into five platoons; when the paralleled but not crossed flags are separated, the formation combined by three will split again into three platoons. When the troops are split, assembling them will be the unorthodox; when the troops are assembled, splitting them will be the unorthodox. After repeated commands and practice of splitting and assembling, they will go back to orthodox training. Then you can start the regular training with the formation deployment method of the 'four heads and eight tails.' This is an appropriate way of formation deployment training."

【原文】

太宗称善。

太宗曰："曹公有战骑、陷骑、游骑，今马军何等比乎？"

靖曰："臣按《新书》云：战骑居前，陷骑居中，游骑居后。如此则是各立名号，分为三类尔。大抵骑队八马，当车徒二十四人；二十四骑，当车徒七十二人。此古制也。车徒常教以正，骑队常教以奇。据曹公，前后及中分为三覆，不言两厢，举一端言也。后人不晓三覆之义，则战骑必前于陷骑、

【今译】

太宗表示赞赏。

唐太宗说："曹操把骑兵分为战骑、陷骑、游骑，我们现在所用的骑兵怎样和它类比？"

李靖说："我根据《曹公新书》上说：战骑在前，陷骑居中，游骑在后。这样便各有名称，分成三类。大体上骑兵的八骑相当于随车步卒二十四人；二十四骑相当于随车步卒七十二人。这是古代定制。对于随车步卒，通常教他们正兵的战术；对于骑兵，通常教他们奇兵的战术。根据曹操的说法，把骑兵部队分作前、中、后三个梯队，没说到左右两翼，是仅就一种部署来说的。后人不明白'三覆'（指骑兵的前、后、中三个梯队灵活运用）的含义，拘泥于战骑一定要摆在陷骑和游骑之前，这样怎能运

Tang Taizong expressed his appreciation.

Tang Taizong said: "Cao Cao divided his cavalry into fighting cavalry, attacking cavalry and roving cavalry. How can we compare them with our contemporary cavalry?"

Li Jing said: "According to the *New Book of Duke Cao*, the fighting cavalry is in the front, the attacking cavalry is in the middle and the roving cavalry is in the rear. Thus they have their own names and are divided into three types. Generally speaking, eight cavalrymen are equivalent to twenty-four infantrymen accompanying the chariot; twenty-four cavalrymen are equivalent to seventy-two infantrymen accompanying the chariot. This was the ancient system. The infantrymen accompanying the chariot should be taught the orthodox tactics and the cavalrymen should be taught the unorthodox tactics. Cao Cao talked about the three cavalry echelons in the front, middle and rear, but he did not speak of the left and right wings, so what he talked about was only one type of deployment. Later generations do not understand the implications of the 'Three Coverings' (referring to the flexible employment of the cavalry echelons in the

【原文】

游骑，如何使用？臣熟用此法，回车转阵，则游骑当前，战骑当后，陷骑临变而分，皆曹公之术也。”

太宗笑曰：“多少人为曹公所惑！”

太宗曰：“车、步、骑三者一法也，其用在人乎？”

靖曰：“臣按春秋鱼丽阵，先偏后伍，此则车步无骑，谓之左右拒，言拒御而已，非取出奇胜也。晋荀吴伐狄，舍车为行，此则骑多为便，唯务奇胜，非拒御而已。臣均其术：凡一马当三人，车步称之，混为一法，用之在人。敌安知吾车果何出，骑果何

【今译】

用得好呢？我常常使用这种办法：只要回军转阵，就使游骑变为前阵，战骑变为后阵，陷骑根据情况变化灵活运用。这都是曹操的用兵之法啊。”

太宗说：“有多少人被曹操的‘三覆’之法迷惑啊！”

唐太宗说：“车兵、步兵、骑兵的运用方法是一致的，那么运用的好坏就在于指挥者了？”

李靖说：“我根据春秋时郑庄公创制的鱼丽阵，把战车摆在前面，步卒分散在战车两翼和后边，这是因为当时只有车兵、步卒而无骑兵，这种阵区分为‘左拒’、‘右拒’，说的是左右两翼拒御敌人而已，并不是出奇制胜。晋荀吴攻打狄人时，曾舍弃车战改为步战，这是方便于用更多的骑兵机动作战，

front, middle and rear), assuming that the fighting cavalry must be placed in front of the attacking cavalry and the roving cavalry, then how can they be well employed? The method I often use is that when the formation is turned about, the roving cavalry will become the front and the fighting cavalry will become the rear, and the attacking cavalry will be used according to the changing situation. These are all Cao Cao's commanding methods."

Tang Taizong said: "How many people have been confused by Cao Cao's art of the 'Three Coverings'!"

Tang Taizong said: "As the method to employ chariots, infantrymen and cavalrymen is the same, does their employment then lie with the commander?"

Li Jing said: "Duke Zhuang of Zheng in the Spring and Autumn Period created the Yu Li Formation. He placed the chariots in the front with the infantrymen dispersed at the flank and behind, because at his time there were only chariots and infantrymen but no cavalrymen. This formation was distinguished as the 'Left Resisting Formation' and the 'Right Resisting For-

【原文】

来，徒果何从哉？或潜九地，或动九天，其知如神，唯陛下有焉，臣何足以知之？”

太宗曰：“太公书云：地方六百步，或六十步，

【今译】

其目的在于出奇制胜，而不是单纯为了防御。我综合了这些办法，以一个骑兵相当三个步兵，同时配备一定数量的车兵和步兵，三者统一编组，由指挥者灵活运用。这样，敌人怎么知道我的战车从哪里杀出，骑兵从哪里来，步卒要攻打哪里？指挥部队作战或者像是藏在九地之下，或者像是动于九天之上，这样用兵如神的智慧，只有陛下您才有这样的才能，我哪里能够知道其中的奥妙呢！”

唐太宗说：“《太公兵法》说：方阵每边上六百步，或者六十步，并依照十二星辰的顺序标示出来。

mation' for the purpose of resisting and defending, not making surprise attacks. When Xun Wu of Jin State attacked the Di tribes, they abandoned the chariots and used infantrymen in order to make more use of the cavalrymen for manoeuver attacks. The purpose of it was for a surprise move and not pure defense. I have combined these methods: use one cavalryman for three infantrymen and have the cavalrymen accompanied by a certain number of chariots and infantrymen;organize the three into one under a unified command and employ them according to the circumstances. Thus how can the enemy know where my chariots will rush forth, where my cavalry men will come out and where my infantrymen will attack? Such miraculous wisdom to command the troops like being hidden as under the most secret recesses of Earth or flashing forth as from above the topmost heights of Heaven is a talent possessed only by Your Majesty, how can I be able to reach its profundity?"

Tang Taizong said: "The *Taigong's Art of War* states: 'Each side of the square formation is six hundred or sixty paces long and is marked in

【原文】

表十二辰。其术如何？”

靖曰：“画地方一千二百步，开方之形也。每部占地二十步之方，横以五步立一人，纵以四步立一人，凡二千五百人。分五方，空地四处，所谓阵间容阵者也。武王伐纣，虎贲各掌三千人，每阵六千人，共三万之众。此太公画地之法也。”

太宗曰：“卿六花阵，画地几何？”

靖曰：“大阅：地方千二百步者，其义六阵，各占地四百步，分为东西两厢，空地一千二百步，

【今译】

其具体方法是怎么样的呢？”

李靖说：“在布阵的区域内画一个正方形方阵，每边为三百步，周长为一千二百步。每个战术小方阵占地是边长为二十步的正方形。每个最小战术单位横向每五步站一人，纵向每四步站一人。二千五百人分为五阵列于东西南北中五方，在方阵四角上有空地四块，这就是所谓大阵包容小阵。周武王讨伐商纣时，命令虎贲之士各率三千人，每阵六千人，五阵共三万人。这是姜太公画地布阵的方法。”

太宗说：“你所创制的六花阵画地多少？”

李靖说：“大规模检阅部队时，全阵每边长一千二百步，包容六个小阵，每小阵占有边长为四百步的正方形，并把六个方阵分为东西两厢，中间空余地带的两条长边是一千二百步，作为教战的场所。

the order of the twelve constellations.' What are the techniques of this?"

Li Jing said: "Draw a square in the area where the formation is about to be deployed. Each side of the square is three hundred paces with a perimeter of one thousand two hundred paces. Each small tactical formation occupies a square of twenty paces long on each side. For every smallest tactical unit, a man is stationed every five paces horizontally and every four paces vertically. Two thousand five hundred men are divided into five formations deployed in the east, west, south, north and center. At the four corners of the square formation, there are four open areas, and this is called 'formation containing formations.' When King Wu of Zhou attacked King Zhou of Shang, he ordered each Tiger Warrior to lead three thousand men with six thousand men in a formation and thirty thousand in five formations all together. This is the way of Taigong to deploy formations by delineating the terrain."

Tang Taizong said: "How do you delineate the terrain for your 'Six Pedals Formation'?"

Li Jing said: "Large-scale manoeuvers are as

【原文】

为教战之所。臣尝教士三万，每阵五千人，以其一为营法，五为方、圆、曲、直、锐之形，每阵五变，凡二十五变而止。”

太宗曰：“五行阵如何？”

靖曰：“本因五方色立此名。方、圆、曲、直、锐，实因地形使然。凡军不素习此五者，安可以临敌乎？兵，诡道也，故强名五行焉，文之以术数相

【今译】

我曾经用士卒三万人进行六花阵的教练，每阵五千人，其中一个方阵演练驻营的方法，其他五阵演练方、圆、曲、直、锐等阵形变化，每阵变化五次，五阵共变化二十五次。”

太宗说：“五行阵又是怎么回事呢？”

李靖说：“五行阵原来是依据五个方位和五种颜色来命名的。方、圆、曲、直、锐五种阵形的变换，实际上是根据不同地形布列的不同阵势。军队如果不熟悉这五种阵形，怎么可以接敌作战呢？用兵打仗就是以诡诈为原则，所以故意以五行之名来

follows: the whole formation, each side being one thousand two hundred paces long, contains six small formations. Every small formation occupies a square with each side of four hundred paces long. The six square formations are divided into eastern and western wings. The central open strip area is one thousand two hundred paces long on each side and is used for training warfare. I once used thirty thousand troops for training in the 'Six Pedals Formation, each formation containing five thousand men. Of the six formations, five practiced the way of encampment and the other five practiced the square, round, curved, straight and angular dispositions. Each formation went through five changes and five formations went through a total of twenty-five changes."

Tang Taizong said: "Then how about the 'Five Elements Formations'?"

Li Jing said: "The 'Five Elements Formations' was originally named after the five quarters and five colors. The changes of the square, round, curved, straight and angular formations are actually different formations deployed according to different terrains. If the army is not

【原文】

生相克之义。其实兵形像水，因地制流，此其旨也。”

太宗曰：“李勣言牝牡、方圆伏兵法，古有是否?”

靖曰：“牝牡之法，出于俗传，其实阴阳二义而已。臣按范蠡云：‘后则用阴，先则用阳。尽敌阳节，盈吾阴节而夺之。’此兵家阴阳之妙也。范蠡又云：‘设右为牝，益左为牡，早晏以顺天道。’此则左右早晏，临时不同，在乎奇正之变者也。左右者，人之阴阳；早晏者，天之阴阳；奇正者，天人

【今译】

命名五行阵，并用五行相克相生的术数意义来文饰它。其实，军队作战时的阵形如同流水一般，像是依照地势的高低决定其流向一样来选定阵形，这才是五行阵的本旨含义。”

唐太宗说：“李勣说牝牡、方圆之中都隐含用兵的法则，古人有这种说法吗?”

李靖说：“牝牡雌雄之法，出于俗传，其实就是军事上讲的阴阳这一对范畴。我根据范蠡所说：‘后则用阴，先则用阳。尽敌阳节，盈吾阴节而夺之。’（后发制人要用潜力，先发制人要用锐气。要完全摧毁敌人的锐气，充分发挥我的潜力消灭敌人）这是军事家讲的运用‘阴’、‘阳’的奥妙。范蠡又说：‘设右为牝，益左为牡，早晏以顺天道。’（布

familiar with these five formations, how can it engage and fight the enemy? All warfare is based on deception. For the same purpose, the 'Five Elements Formations' is named after the five elements and described on the principle of the five elements producing and overcoming each other. But in actuality, the form of an army in war is like water which changes its course in accordance with the contours of the land. This is what the 'Five Elements Formations' really implies."

Tang Taizong said: "Li Ji said that female and male, square and round all contain rules of warfare. Did the ancients ever speak about that?"

Li Jing said: "The female and male rules come out of the popular circulation. In fact, they refer to the concept of *Yin* and *Yang* in the military. Fan Li said: 'Rely on potentialities (*Yin*) to subdue the enemy when striking after he has struck; and subdue the enemy with driving force (*Yang*) when striking first. The enemy's driving force should be completely destroyed and our potentialities should be exploited to its full to annihilate the enemy.' This is the secrecy of the

【原文】

相变之阴阳。若执而不变，则阴阳俱废。如何？守牝牡之形而已。故形之者，以奇示敌，非吾正也；胜之者，以正击敌，非吾奇也。此谓奇正相变。兵伏者，不止山谷草木伏藏，所以为伏也，其正如山，

【今译】

设在右方的为牝阵，加强在左方的为牡阵。行动的早晚要顺应天时变化的规律）这里说的布阵左右、早晚，因时机而有所不同，这就在乎奇正变化了。左右是指人的阴阳，早晚是指天的阴阳，奇正是指天、人相变的阴阳，如果拘泥不变，那么阴阳相变就失去了意义，只剩下空守牝牡的形式。所以，伪装和佯动的方法是，用奇兵当作正兵去迷惑敌人，而实际上并不是我的正兵；战胜敌人的方法是用正兵当作奇兵打击敌人，而实际上并不是我的奇兵。这就是所谓的奇正相互变化。所谓的伏兵并不仅仅是指利用山谷草木的有利条件藏伏隐蔽部队，真正的伏兵，是指运用正兵时能像山岳般雄稳不可摧，

application of *Yin* and *Yang* according to strategists. Fan Li also said: 'The formation deployed on the right is female and the one strengthened on the left is male. Whether an action should be taken early or late should be decided according to the change of the seasons and climate.' Thus left and right, early and late are different according to the timing. They lie in the changes of the unorthodox and orthodox. Left and right refer to the *Yin* and *Yang* in man, early and late refer to the *Yin* and *Yang* in nature. The unorthodox and orthodox refer to the mutual transformation of *Yin* and *Yang* in nature and man. If one denies the change, the mutual transformation of *Yin* and *Yang* will then lose its importance, leaving an empty form of female and male for him to hold on to. Thus the way to feint and delude the enemy is to use the unorthodox forces as the orthodox forces in order to confuse the enemy, while such in actuality are not our orthodox forces; the way to conquer the enemy is to use the orthodox forces as unorthodox forces to attack him while such in actuality are not our unorthodox forces. This is called 'mutual change of the unorthodox and orthodox.' The forces in ambush do not

【原文】

其奇如雷，敌虽对面，莫测吾奇正所在。至此，夫何形之有焉？”

太宗曰：“四兽之阵，又以商、羽、徵、角象之，何道也？”

靖曰：“诡道也。”

太宗曰：“可废乎？”

靖曰：“存之，所以能废之也。若废而不用，诡愈甚焉。”

太宗曰：“何谓也？”

【今译】

运用奇兵时能像雷霆般迅疾凌厉。敌人虽然近在对面，也没法弄清我方哪里是正、哪里是奇。如果奇正运用达到如此程度，那么奇正变化哪里还会有形迹可寻呢？”

唐太宗说：“鸟、龟、龙、虎四兽之阵，又用商、羽、徵、角四音来表示，这是为什么呢？”

李靖说：“这是兵家的诡诈之道。”

太宗说：“可以废除吗？”

李靖说：“保存它，就是为了能废除它。如果废除，不用它，反而会使诡诈之术越弄越玄虚。”

太宗说：“这怎么说？”

mean the forces lying in ambush and hiding in the mountains, valleys, grass and trees. The true meaning of ambush is to have our orthodox forces holding their position rock firm as a mountain, and our unorthodox forces striking like thunder. Although the enemy is close to our front, he will not tell which is our orthodox force and which is our unorthodox force. If one employs the unorthodox and orthodox to such an extent, then how can the change of unorthodox and orthodox leave any trace to follow?"

Tang Taizong said: "The four animal formations of bird, turtle, dragon and tiger have also the four musical notes of Shang, Yu, Zheng and Jue (notes of the ancient Chinese five-tone scale) to represent them, what is the reason for this?"

Li Jing said: "It is the way of military deceit."

Tang Taizong said: "Can they be dispensed with?"

Li Jing said: "When you preserve them, you will then be able to dispense with them. If you dispense with them and do not use them, deceitfulness will grow ever greater."

Tang Taizong said: "What do you mean by this?"

【原文】

靖曰："假之以四兽之阵，及天、地、风、云之号，又加商金、羽水、徵火、角木之配，此皆兵家自古诡道。存之，则余诡不复增矣；废之，则使贪使愚之术从何而施哉？"

太宗良久曰："卿宜秘之，无泄于外。"

太宗曰："严刑峻法，使人畏我而不畏敌，朕甚惑之。昔光武以孤军当王莽百万之众，非有刑法临之，此何由乎？"

靖曰："兵家胜败，情状万殊，不可以一事推

【今译】

李靖说："假借鸟、龟、龙、虎四兽的阵名，以及天、地、风、云的名号，又加上商金、羽水、徵火、角木的相互匹配，这是兵家自古以来的诡秘方法。保留这些名称就不会增加更加诡秘的名称了；如果将其废除，那么驱使贪婪、愚昧的人又能用别的什么办法呢？"

太宗沉思良久，说："你要保守秘密，不要泄露出去。"

唐太宗说："用严刑峻法会使官兵畏惧我而不畏惧敌人，对这个说法我心里深感疑惑。从前汉光武帝以一支孤立无援的军队抵当王莽的百万大军，这并不是用严刑峻法来迫使部队与敌人作战的。这是什么原因？"

李靖说："兵家胜败，情况千差万别，不能用一件事例去推断。比如陈胜、吴广打败秦朝军队，

Li Jing said: "They were named after the four animals of bird, turtle, dragon and tiger together with the designations of Heaven, Earth, wind and cloud and represented with the associated phrases of Shang Jin (metal), Yu Shui (water), Zheng Huo (fire) and Jue Mu (wood). This was the way of ancient military strategists to obscure things. If you preserve these names, there will not be any more obscured names for them; if you abandon them, how can the greedy and stupid be employed?"

Tang Taizong thought for a long while and said: "You must keep this a secret and never let it be leaked outside."

Tang Taizong said: "Severe punishments and strict laws make men fear me and not the enemy. I am very doubtful about this. In the past, Emperor Guangwu of the Han Dynasty resisted Wang Mang's army of one million men with a solitary force and he did not force his men to fight the enemy with severe punishments and strict laws. How could he be victorious?"

Li Jing said: "An army's victory or defeat is decided by a myriad factors and should not be inferred from one case alone. For example, when

【原文】

也。如陈胜、吴广败秦师，岂胜、广刑法能加于秦乎？光武之起，盖顺人心之怨莽也，况又王寻、王邑不晓兵法，徒夸兵众，所以自败。臣按《孙子》曰：‘卒未亲附而罚之，则不服；已亲附，而罚不行，则不可用。’此言凡将先有爱结于士，然后可以严刑也。若爱未加而独用峻法，鲜克济焉。”

太宗曰：“《尚书》言：‘威克厥爱，允济；爱克厥威，允罔功。’何谓也？”

【今译】

难道是陈胜吴广的刑罚比秦朝的刑罚更严酷吗？汉光武帝当初的兴起，是因为顺应了广大民众心怨王莽的形势，更何况王莽将领王寻、王邑等人不懂兵法，光会自夸人多势众，所以自取败亡。我根据《孙子兵法》所说：‘卒未亲附而罚之，则不服；已亲附，而罚不行，则不可用。’（士卒还没有亲近依附就执行惩罚，那么他们就会不服，不服就很难使用。士卒已经亲近依附，如果仍不执行军纪军法，也不能用来作战）这些话的意思是，将领首先要爱抚士兵，然后才可执行严厉的刑罚。如果没有爱抚士兵而单独使用严刑峻法去约束士兵，那是很少能奏效的。”

太宗说：“《尚书》里说的‘威克厥爱，允济；爱克厥威，允罔功。’（威严胜过爱抚，事情可以成功；爱抚超过威严，事情就不会成功）这怎么解释呢？”

Chen Sheng and Wu Guang defeated the Qin army, was it because they had more severe punishments than those of Qin? The rise of Emperor Guangwu of Han was probably due to his according with the people's hatred for Wang Mang. Moreover, Wang Mang's general Wang Xun and Wang Yi did not know military strategy and only boasted about their big numbers of troops. So it was not surprising that they were defeated. *Sun Zi's Art of War* says: 'If troops are punished before they have grown attached to you, they will be disobedient. If they are not obedient, it is difficult to employ them. If troops have become attached to you, but discipline is not enforced, you cannot employ them either.' This means that a general should first pay tender attention to and care for his soldiers before employing severe punishments. Without such attention and care, mere severe punishments and strict laws will not achieve intended results."

Tang Taizong said: "*The Collection of Ancient Texts* states that 'when awesomeness exceeds love, one will be successful; when love exceeds awesomeness, one will not be successful.' How do you explain this?"

【原文】

靖曰："爱设于先，威设于后，不可反是也。若威加于前，爱救于后，无益于事矣。《尚书》所以慎戒其终，非所以作谋于始也。故《孙子》之法万代不刊。"

太宗曰："卿平萧铣，诸将皆欲籍伪臣家以赏士卒，独卿不从，以谓蒯通不戮于汉，既而江汉归顺。朕由是思古人有言曰：'文能附众，武能威敌'，其卿之谓乎？"

靖曰："汉光武平赤眉，入贼营中案行。贼曰：

【今译】

李靖说："先用爱抚，后用刑罚，这是不可颠倒的。如果先用刑罚，后用爱抚，那样无益于事。《尚书》所说是告诫人们要重视刑罚、注意后果，而不是说刑罚要作为先于爱抚的教育原则。所以，《孙子兵法》的原则是万代不能更改的。"

唐太宗说："爱卿当年平定萧铣时，众将领都主张没收萧铣及其属下的财产赏赐士卒，惟独你不同意，并用历史上刘邦不杀蒯通的例子来说服大家，不久收到江汉流域萧铣势力全部归顺我朝的效果。朕由此联想到古人说过的：'文能附众，武能威敌'(政治才能可以争取群众，军事才能足以慑服敌人)，这不是在说你吗？"

李靖说："汉光武帝平定赤眉军之后，骑马进入赤眉军营中，按辔缓行。赤眉军兵士们议论说：

Li Jing said: "First love then punishments, this cannot be reverted. If punishments are employed before love, it will be of no good. What is said in *The Collection of Ancient Texts* is to warn people that more attention should be paid to the effects although punishment is also very important. It does not say that first punishment then love is an educational principle. So, the ideas contained in *Sun Zi's Art of War* cannot be changed even for ten thousand generations."

Tang Taizong said: "When you conquered Xiao Xian, all the generals wanted to confiscate the properties of his and his subordinates' to reward the troops, only you disagreed and talked them into agreement with a case in history where Kuai Tong was not executed by Liu Bang. Soon after, Xiao Xian's forces in the basin of the Yangtse and Han rivers all submitted to us. From this I recalled the ancient saying that 'good at government, you will attract the masses; good at warfare, you will overawe the enemy.' Isn't this referred to you?"

Li Jing said: "When Emperor Guangwu of Han conquered the Red Eyebrows, he entered the Red Eyebrows' encampment and walked

【原文】

'萧王推赤心于人腹中。'此盖先料人情本非为恶，岂不豫虑哉！臣顷讨突厥，总番汉之众，出塞千里，未尝戮一杨(扬)干，斩一庄贾，亦推赤诚存至公而已矣。陛下过听，擢臣以不次之位，若于文武则何敢当！"

太宗曰："昔唐俭使突厥，卿因击而败之。人言卿以俭为死间，朕至今疑焉。如何？"

靖再拜曰："臣与俭比肩事主，料俭说必不能

【今译】

'萧王这次来对我们真是推心置腹、坦诚相见。'这是因为刘秀事前估计到赤眉军并不都是与他为敌的，哪里是他预先没有考虑过有没有危险？我不久前征讨突厥，统率汉族和少数民族兵马出塞千里，没有诛杀一个像扬干那样的人，也没有斩杀一个像庄贾那样的人，也是推诚待人，秉公办事而已。陛下过分信任我，把我擢升到很高的位置，如果说我文武兼备，就实在不敢当了！"

唐太宗说："当年派遣唐俭出使突厥，你乘他与突厥头领会见的机会以突然袭击的方式打败突厥。人们都说这是你把唐俭当成死间来用。朕至今怀疑这种议论。这是怎么一回事呢？"

李靖再拜而后回答说："臣与唐俭一起辅佐君主，目的是相同的。我料定唐俭不可能以言辞说服

slowly on his horse. The Red Eyebrows soldiers said: 'King Xiao (Emperor Guangwu) is really straightforward and honest toward us.' That is probably because Liu Xiu (Emperor Guangwu) had previously evaluated the Red Eyebrows as not all opposing him but it does not mean that he did not anticipate any danger. Not long ago, I led a combined force of both Han and minority troops for an expedition against the Turks. I traveled a thousand *li* and did not kill a single man like Yang Gan and did not behead a single man like Zhuang Jia. This, too, was due to frankness and impartiality. Your Majesty trusts me very much and has put me onto such a high position, but as for what you say about my excelling both at government and military commanding, I really do not deserve it."

Tang Taizong said: "Formerly, when Tang Jian was sent on a diplomatic mission to Turk, you took the chance of his meeting with the Turk leaders and defeated the Turks by a surprise attack. People say that you used Tang Jian as an 'expendable spy.' Up until now I still have doubts about this. How do you explain it?"

Li Jing bowed again and said: "Tang Jian and

【原文】

柔服，故臣因纵兵击之，所以去大恶不顾小义也。人谓以俭为死间，非臣之心。按《孙子》，用间最为下策，臣尝著论其末云：水能载舟，亦能覆舟。或用间以成功，或凭间以倾败。若束发事君，当朝正色，忠以尽节，信以竭诚，虽有善间，安可用乎？唐俭小义，陛下何疑？”

太宗曰：“诚哉！非仁义不能使间，此岂纤人

【今译】

突厥，所以才乘机出兵袭击突厥。这样为铲除国家大患就顾不上个人之间的小义了。人们说我把唐俭当成死间去运用，这决不是我的本意。《孙子》说过用间是最下策，我曾经在《用间篇》的后边批注说：‘水能载舟，也能覆舟。既有因为用间而获得成功的，也有因为用间而招致失败的。’我从年轻时起就辅佐君主，在参与朝政中公正坦直，忠心耿耿以尽臣节，信实无欺竭诚待人，虽然有善于离间你我君臣关系的人，又怎么能起作用呢？唐俭的事，只是私人之间的小义，陛下何必怀疑？”

太宗说：“的确是这样啊！不是宽怀仁义的人是不能使用间谍的，这岂是卑俗小人所能做到的呢？

I both served Your Majesty for the same purpose. I believed that Tang Jian's proposals could not persuade the Turks to submit, so I took the opportunity and attacked the Turks. In order to eliminate a great danger for our state, I just could not think too much about the minor righteousness. People say that I used Tang Jian as an expendable spy. It was really not my intention. Sun Zi said that to use spies is an inferior resort. I annotated Sun Zi's *Use of Spies* that 'Water can float a boat and can also overturn it. There were successful cases of using spies and there were also cases when using spies led to defeat.' I started to serve Your Majesty when I was young. I have been impartial and straight in managing court affairs. I am loyal as a court official and faithful, honest and sincere to others. Although there are people who like to sow dissension between Your Majesty and me, how can they succeed? What happened to Tang Jian was only a matter of minor righteousness between him and me. Your Majesty should not have any doubt of it."

Tang Taizong said: "Indeed! Only those who are benevolent and righteous are able to use

【原文】

所为乎？周公大义灭亲，况一使人乎？灼无疑矣！”

太宗曰：“兵贵为主，不贵为客；贵速，不贵久。何也？”

靖曰：“兵，不得已而用之，安在为客且久哉？《孙子》曰：‘远输则百姓贫’，此为客之弊也。又曰：‘役不再籍，粮不三载’，此不可久之验也。臣较量主客之势，则有变客为主、变主为客之术。”

太宗曰：“何谓也？”

【今译】

周公为大义而灭亲，何况唐俭只是一个使臣呢。现在我明白无疑了。”

唐太宗说：“用兵作战，贵为主，不贵为客；贵速胜，不贵持久。这是为什么呢？”

李靖说：“战争是不得已而为之的事情，怎么可以既采取进攻又久拖不决呢？《孙子兵法》说：‘远输则百姓贫’（军队远征，远道运输，就会使百姓世族贫困），说的是作战时处在‘客’的位置上的不利之处。《孙子兵法》又说：‘役不再籍，粮不三载’（善于用兵打仗的人，兵员不再次征集，粮秣不多次运送），这是战争不应久拖的经验。我曾考究过攻防双方有利不利的态势，可以找到变我不利为有利、变敌有利为不利的方法。”

太宗说：“是什么样的办法？”

spies. How can a lowly and ordinary man do it? The Duke of Zhou could exterminate his relatives for the great righteousness, let alone Tang Jian who was only an emissary. I do not have any doubt now."

Tang Taizong said: "What is valued in war is to be the 'host' (to be initiative) and not the 'guest' (to be passive) and to win a quick victory and not to conduct prolonged operations. Why?"

Li Jing said: "War is something that has to be done when there are no other choices, so how can attacks be prolonged? *Sun Zi's Art of War* says: 'Being forced to carry supplies for great distances will render the people destitute.' It refers to the disadvantages of an army to be a guest in a war. *Sun Zi's Art of War* also says: 'Do not ask for a second levy of conscripts or more than three provisionings.' This is an advice of not to have a war last long. I once studied the advantages and disadvantages of the offensive and the defensive and found a way to change our disadvantages into advantages and the enemy's advantages into disadvantages."

Tang Taizong said: "What is it?"

【原文】

靖曰："'因粮于敌'，是变客为主也；'饱能饥之，佚能劳之'，是变主为客也。故兵不拘主客迟速，唯发必中节，所以为宜。"

太宗曰："古人有诸？"

靖曰："昔越伐吴，以左右二军鸣鼓而进，吴分兵御之。越以中军潜涉不鼓，袭败吴师，此变客为主之验也。石勒与姬澹战，澹兵远来，勒遣孔苌

【今译】

李靖说："'因粮于敌'（粮秣取用于敌国），就是反客为主；'饱能饥之，佚能劳之'（敌人粮秣充足时设法使它挨饿，敌人休整安逸时设法使它疲惫），就是变主为客。所以用兵作战不在乎防守进攻、缓战速决，只要是指挥作战恰到好处，那就是正确的。"

太宗问道："古人有这方面的例子吗？"

李靖说："从前越王勾践伐吴，用左右两军击鼓而进，吴军分兵抵挡。越军以中军停止敲鼓隐蔽潜渡笠泽，发起突然袭击，打败吴国军队。这是变客为主的例子。西晋末年石勒与姬澹作战，姬澹率兵远来，石勒派孔苌为前锋迎击姬澹的军队。孔苌

Li Jing said: " 'To make up for the provisions relying on the enemy' is to turn from a guest to a host; 'to try to starve a well-fed enemy and to try to exhaust a resting enemy' is to turn from a host to a guest. So the army is not confined to being offensive or defensive, conducting prolonged operations or striving for a quick victory as long as the operations are appropriately commanded. It is correct."

Tang Taizong said: "Do we have any ancient examples on this?"

Li Jing said: "In antiquity, when King Goujian of Yue State attacked the state of Wu, his forces on the left and right beat their drums and advanced. When Wu divided its forces to resist, the central force of Yue stopped sounding their drums and secretly forded the river of Li Ze. They launched a surprise attack and defeated Wu's army. This is an example of turning a guest into a host. In the later years of the Western Jin Dynasty, when Shi Le was at war with Ji Dan, Ji Dan came from afar. Shi Le dispatched Kong Chang as the forward to resist Ji Dan's army. Kong Chang withdrew deliberately. Ji Dan pursued, and then was attacked by Shi Le's

【原文】

为前锋，逆击澹军，孔苌退而澹来追，勒以伏兵夹击之，澹军大败，此变劳为佚之验也。古人如此者多。”

太宗曰：“铁蒺藜、行马，太公所制，是乎?”

靖曰：“有之，然拒敌而已。兵贵致人，非欲拒之也。太公《六韬》言守御之具尔，非攻战所施也。”

【今译】

故意退却来吸引姬澹追击，石勒用伏兵夹击姬澹的追击部队，结果姬澹大败。这是变劳为逸的经验。古人这种事例是很多的。”

唐太宗说：“铁蒺藜和行马，据说是姜太公创制的，是这样吗?”

李靖说：“有这么回事，然而这只是单纯为了抵御敌人而已。用兵作战贵在能够调动敌人，而不仅仅是能阻止和顶住敌人。太公《六韬》上讲到的铁蒺藜、行马只是守御的工具，而不是进攻作战时使用的东西。”

ambush force and suffered a disastrous defeat. This is a case of changing the tired into the rested. The ancients had many cases like this."

Tang Taizong said: "The caltrops and chevaux-de-frise are said to be created by Jiang Taigong. Is it true?"

Li Jing said: "It is true. But they were created only for resisting the enemy. What is valued in a war is not merely how to stop and resist the enemy but how to have him move in your direction. The caltrops and chevaux-de-frise mentioned in the Six Stratagies of Jiang Taigong were equipment for defense only and not for attack."

卷下

【原文】

太宗曰："太公云：'以步兵与车骑战者，必依丘墓险阻。'又孙子云：'天隙之地，丘墓故城，兵不可处。'如何？"

靖曰："用众在乎心一；心一在乎禁祥去疑。倘主将有所疑忌，则群情摇；群情摇，则敌乘衅而

【今译】

太宗说："太公《六韬》说：'用步兵迎战车兵和骑兵，一定要依托丘陵、墓地和险阻。'可是《孙子兵法》又说：'对天然形成的雨裂深沟、丘陵墓地及废墟等地形，军队不要停驻。'这怎么解释？"

李靖说："指挥部队作战关键在于全军上下统一意志；统一意志的关键在于禁止迷信、破除疑虑。倘若主将有所疑忌，那么军心就会动摇；军心动摇，敌人就会乘隙而入。安营扎寨、坚守阵地，要能方便军

BOOK III

Tang Taizong said: "Taigong's *Six Stratagies* says: 'When infantrymen engage the chariots and cavalrymen in battle, they must take advantage of hills, tomb mounds and rugged steeps and defiles.' But *Sun Zi's Art of War* also says: 'Forces should not be situated in places like ravines, hills, tomb mounds and old ruins.' Why?"

Li Jing said: "The key to employing troops in battle is to unify their minds and the key to the unification of minds is to prohibit superstition and dispel doubts. If the commanding general has doubts, the morale of the troops will be sapped and if the morale is sapped, the enemy will take the opportunity to sneak in. Setting up camps and holding positions must be convenient for the army to manoeuver. Terrains like deep ravines, 'Heavenly Wells,' 'Heavenly Falls,' 'Heavenly Cracks,' 'Heavenly Prisons' and 'Heavenly Nets' are not convenient for an army

【原文】

至矣。安营据地，便乎人事而已。若涧、井、陷、隙之地，及如牢如罗之处，人事不便者也，故兵家引而避之，防敌乘我。丘墓故城，非绝险处，我得之为利，岂宜反去之乎？太公所说，兵之至要也！”

太宗曰：“朕思，凶器无甚于兵者。行兵苟便于人事，岂以避忌为疑？今后诸将有以阴阳拘忌失于事宜者，卿当丁宁诫之。”

靖再拜谢曰：“臣按《尉缭子》云：黄帝以德守之，以刑伐之，是谓刑德，非天官日时之谓也。

【今译】

队行动。像深涧、天井、天陷、天隙以及天牢、天罗等地形，不便于军队行动，所以兵家都要引兵而去，避开这种地方，防止敌人乘机袭我。至于那些丘陵、墓地及废墟，不是险不可近的地方，我们如果先敌占领，那会有利于战斗，怎么能离而远去呢？太公所说的是用兵中最重要的原则。”

太宗说：“我想，最凶险的事情没有超过战争的，只要有利于军队行动，怎么能因为避讳禁忌的邪说而犹豫不决呢？今后，众将领中如果有人拘泥于阴阳术数而导致贻误军机的，你应当耐心叮嘱反复告诫他们。”

李靖再拜之后称谢说：“根据《尉缭子》的说法，黄帝以仁德治理天下，以武力讨伐敌人。这就是古人所说的刑德，而不是阴阳术数家们所说的天

to manoeuver. Therefore, strategists tend to stay away and try to avoid such places so as to prevent the enemy from taking the advantage to attack us. As for the hills and tomb mounds, they are not places too dangerous to approach. If we take them before the enemy, they will be places good for combat. Why should we stay away from them? What Taigong said was the most important principles of military operations."

Tang Taizong said: "I think that nothing is more violent and dangerous than war. So, we must go ahead with whatever proved advantageous to military operations. How can we be hesitant only because of some evil omens? From now on, if you find any of our generals so confined to the *Yin* and *Yang* techniques as to have forfeited the chance for combat, you should repeatedly and patiently warn and exhort them."

Li Jing bowed his thanks again and said: "According to the *Wei Liao Zi:* 'The Yellow Emperor governed All Under Heaven with benevolence and virtue and used force against his enemy. This is the punishment and virtue referred to by ancients but not the auspicious seasons and

【原文】

然诡道可使由之，不可使知之。后世庸将泥于术数，吴(是)以多败，不可不诫也。陛下圣训，臣即宣告诸将。”

太宗曰：“兵，有分有聚，各贵适宜。前代事迹，孰为善此者？”

靖曰：“苻坚总百万之众，而败于淝水，此兵能合不能分之所致也。吴汉讨公孙述，与副将刘尚分屯，相去二十里，述来攻汉，尚出合击，大破之，

【今译】

官时日。然而诡诈之道可以让人们去做，而不可以让人们知道为什么要那样去做。后代的庸将们拘泥于阴阳术数，因此多有失败，这是不能不引以为诫的。陛下的圣明训示，我将马上宣告诸将。”

唐太宗说：“用兵作战有时要分散使用兵力，有时又要集中使用兵力，贵在根据实际情况灵活处置。以前的战例中，谁最善于运用分散和集中兵力的原则呢？”

李靖说：“苻坚统领百万大军，却在淝水大败，这是因为他用兵过于集中使用，未能分散使用兵力的缘故。东汉将领吴汉征讨公孙述时，与副将刘尚分兵屯驻，两营相距二十里。当公孙述来攻吴汉时，

days referred to by the *Yin* and *Yang* methodologists.' The method of deception, as a matter of fact, will make people do something but will not allow them to understand why they should do it. In later ages, the incompetent generals confined themselves to the techniques of *Yin* and *Yang* and for that reason many suffered defeat. This is a lesson that must be learned. I will immediately announce Your Majesty's sagely instructions to all the generals."

Tang Taizong said: "At war, sometimes one needs to divide his forces and sometimes to reassemble them. It depends on the actual need based on the changing situation. Of the records of earlier cases, who excelled at the tactics of dividing and reassembling the forces?"

Li Jing said: "Fu Jian had an army of a million men but was defeated at the Feishui River. This was because he only used his forces in a reassembled way and did not divide them. When General Wu Han of the Eastern Han Dynasty was on a punitive expedition against Gongsun Shu, he separated from his assistant general Liu Shang and encamped their forces twenty *li* apart. When Gongsun Shu attacked Wu Han, Liu

【原文】

此兵分而能合之所致也。太公云：‘分不分，为縻军；聚不聚，为孤旅。’”

太宗曰：“然。苻坚初得王猛，实知兵，遂取中原；及猛卒，坚果败。此縻军之谓乎？吴汉为光武所任，兵不遥制，故汉果平蜀。此不陷孤旅之谓乎？得失事迹，足为万代鉴！”

太宗曰：“朕观千章万句，不出乎‘多方以误之’一句而已。”

【今译】

刘尚出兵与吴汉合击公孙述，打败了公孙述的部队。这是用兵既能分又能合的结果。姜太公说：‘分不分，为縻军；聚不聚，为孤旅。’（应当分散使用而分散不开的，就是被束缚的军队；应当集中使用而集中不起来的，就是孤立无援的军队）”

太宗说：“是这样的。苻坚最初任用王猛，他还是懂得用兵之道的，所以夺取了中原；等王猛去世之后，苻坚果然失败了。这就是所谓的‘縻军’所致吧！吴汉受到光武帝的信任，指挥作战不受遥控，所以最后平定了西蜀。这就是没有陷入‘孤军’的结果吧！历史上的成败得失，完全可以作为世世代代的借鉴！”

唐太宗说：“我看兵书上尽管有千言万语，其道理都没有超出‘多方以误之’（采取各种办法，造成敌人的失误）这句话的。”

Shang united with Wu Han and defeated Gongsun Shu in a pincer attack. This is the result that an army divides while can also be used reassembled. Jiang Taigong said: 'An army that should divide but does not is an entangled army; an army that should reassemble but does not is a solitary army.'"

Tang Taizong said: "Yes. When Fu Jian employed Wang Meng who knew how to command an army, he took the Central Plains. When Wang Meng died, Fu Jian was defeated as expected. So this might be what is meant by the 'entangled army.' Wu Han was trusted by Emperor Guangwu and was not remotely controlled while directing the war, so he pacified the Western Shu region. This may be the result that his army did not fall into a 'solitary army.' The historical records of gains and losses are sufficient to be used for reference from generation to generation."

Tang Taizong said: "I observe that of the innumerable sentences and words in all the military books, none has gone beyond the statement that 'Use various methods to cause the enemy to make mistakes'."

【原文】

靖良久曰："诚如圣语。大凡用兵，若敌人不误，则我师安能克哉？譬如弈棋，两敌均焉，一着或失，竟莫能救。是古今胜败，率由一误而已，况多失者乎！"

太宗曰："攻守二事，其实一法欤？《孙子》言：'善攻者，敌不知其所守；善守者，敌不知其所攻。'即不言敌来攻我，我亦攻之；我若自守，敌亦守之。攻守两齐，其术奈何？"

靖曰："前代似此相攻相守者多矣，皆曰'守

【今译】

李靖沉默许久，说："确实如陛下所说。大凡用兵，如果敌人没有失误，我军怎么能够取胜呢？如同下棋，双方势均力敌，这时只要有一着失误，就会满盘皆输，无从抢救。所以说古往今来的胜利与失败，大都是由一着失误所造成的，更何况有多次失误的呢！"

唐太宗说："攻和守这两种作战形式，其实同是用以制胜的方法吗？《孙子兵法》说：'善攻者，敌不知其所守；善守者，敌不知其所攻。'（善于进攻的，使敌人不知道怎么防守；善于防守的，使敌人不知道怎么进攻）即使没讲敌人进攻我，我也去进攻它；我若是防守，敌人也防守。双方相攻相守，用什么办法取胜呢？"

李靖说："历史上像这样相攻相守的事例挺多，都说'守则不足，攻则有余'。于是有人认为，这里

After a long while, Li Jing said: "Yes, it is just as Your Majesty said. Generally in military operations, if the enemy does not make any mistakes, how can we conquer him? It is just like playing a chess game where the two players are equal in strength. Either of them makes a mistake, and the whole game will be lost and there will be no rescue to it. So we say that in both ancient and modern times, most of the victories and defeats are decided by a single mistake, let alone many mistakes!"

Tang Taizong said: "Attacking and defending are actually two in one as a method of warfare to conquer the enemy. *Sun Zi's Art of War* says: 'One who excels at attacking makes the enemy unable to know how to defend; one who excels at defending makes the enemy unable to know how to attack.' But it does not speak about the enemy attacking me and me also attacking him, neither about both of us taking a defensive position. If both sides assume the same posture as of mutual attack and mutual defense, what techniques should be employed then?"

Li Jing said: "There are many cases in history of this mutual attack and mutual defense. In all

【原文】

则不足，攻则有余’。便谓不足为弱，有余为强，盖不悟攻守之法也。臣按《孙子》云：‘不可胜者，守也；可胜者，攻也。’谓敌未可胜，则我且自守；待敌可胜，则攻之尔。非以强弱为辞也。后人不晓其义，则当攻而守，当守而攻。二役既殊，故不能一其法。”

太宗曰：“信乎，有余不足，使后人惑其强弱！殊不知守之法，要在示敌以不足；攻之法，要在示

【今译】

的‘不足’就是弱，‘有余’就是强，其实没有完全领会攻守的方法。我按《孙子兵法》所说‘不可胜者，守也；可胜者，攻也。’就是说，还没有战胜敌人的可能时，我暂时采取守势；当有战胜敌人可能的时机出现时，就采取进攻。这并不是就力量的强弱而言的。后人不明白它的真义，以致在应当进攻时反而防守，在应当防守时反而进攻。机械地把攻守两种战法截然分开，所以不能把二者统一起来。”

太宗说：“确实是这样。‘有余’、‘不足’这两个概念使后人疑为力量的强弱了。殊不知，防守的要则是向敌人伪装自己力量不足；进攻的要则是向敌人伪装自己力量有余。对敌人伪装自己力量不

these cases, people would say: 'One takes a defensive position when his strength is inadequate and attacks when the strength is abundant.' Thus someone would think that 'being inadequate' here means that one is weak and 'being abundant' here means that one is strong. Apparently, they did not really understand the methods for attack and defense. I observe *Sun Zi's Art of War* that 'one who can not conquer the enemy assumes a defensive posture; one who can conquer the enemy attacks.' It means that if there is no possibility to conquer the enemy, you must take a defensive position temporarily; when the opportunity to conquer the enemy occurs, you should attack him. This is not a statement about strength and weakness. People of later ages did not understand its meaning, so when they should attack they defended, and when they should defend they attacked. They mechanically separated the two methods of attack and defense, and failed to unite them into one."

Tang Taizong said: "That is true. 'Being abundant' and 'being inadequate' have been mistaken by people of later ages as being strong and being weak. What they did not understand

【原文】

敌以有余也。示敌以不足，则敌必来攻，此是敌不知其所攻者也；示敌以有余，则敌必自守，此是敌不知其所守者也。攻守一决(法)，敌与我分为二事。若我事得，则敌事败；敌事得，则我事败。得失成败，彼我之事分焉。攻守者，一而已矣，得一者百战百胜。故曰‘知彼知己，百战不殆’，其知一之谓乎？”

【今译】

足，则敌人必然要来进攻，这就使敌人不知道它不应当进攻；对敌人伪装自己力量的有余，则敌人必然采取防守，这就使敌人不知道它不应当防守。攻与守虽然是相互对立统一的方法，但在敌我双方来说就分成一攻一守两件事了。如果我运用得当，敌人就会失败；敌人运用得当，那就是我会失败。从战争得失成败的结局来看，就可以分辨出敌我运用攻守方法的好坏了。攻和守不过是一种制胜方法罢了，掌握这种方法就能百战百胜。所以说‘知彼知己，百战不殆’，说的就是对立统一的道理吧。”

was that the essence of defense is to make the enemy believe that your strength is inadequate and the essence of attack is to make the enemy believe that your strength is abundant. When the enemy is made to believe that your strength is inadequate, he will certainly come to attack while unaware that he should not attack. When the enemy is made to believe that your strength is abundant, he will take up defensive positions while unaware that he should not do that. Attacking and defending are a unified method of opposites, but between the enemy and us, they are two separate matters of either attacking or defending. If we employ the method well, the enemy will be defeated, if the enemy employs it well, then it will be us who will be defeated. Whether it is employed well or not either by us or by the enemy will be seen from the gain and loss, success and failure of a war. Attacking and defending are but a way to conquer the enemy. If you excel at them, you will be ever victorious.So we say: 'Know the enemy and know yourself, and you can fight a hundred battles with no danger of defeat.' This refers to the law of unity of opposites, does it not?"

【原文】

靖再拜曰："深乎，圣人之法也！攻是守之机，守是攻之策，同归乎胜而已矣。若攻不知守，守不知攻，不惟二其事，抑又二其官，虽口诵《孙》、《吴》，而心不思妙，攻守两齐之说，其孰能知其然哉？"

太宗曰："《司马法》言：'国虽大，好战必亡；天下虽平(安)，亡(忘)战必危。'此亦攻守一道乎？"

靖曰："有国有家者，曷尝不讲乎攻守也？夫

【今译】

李靖再拜说："深奥啊，古代圣人的用兵之法！进攻是防守的转机，防守是进攻的手段，二者的目的都是为了夺取胜利。如果在进攻中不知道运用防守，防守中不知道运用进攻，这就不仅把进攻和防守完全割裂开，还把进攻和防守的运用各自孤立起来了。一些人虽然能背诵孙子、吴子的兵法，但不能领悟其运用上的奥妙，他怎么能明白攻、守密不可分的深刻道理呢？"

唐太宗说："《司马法》说：'国虽大，好战必亡；天下虽安，忘战必危。'（国家虽大，好战必定灭亡；天下虽然安定，忘掉战备必有危险）这也是讲攻守统一的道理吗？"

李靖说："凡是有国有家的，怎么能不讲求攻守呢？进攻，不仅要能攻打敌人的城池和战阵，还

Li Jing bowed again and said: "How profound are these methods of warfare of the ancient sages! Attacking is a turn of defense and defense is a means for attack, both aiming at winning victory. If in attacking you do not know how to defend, and in defending how to attack, you not only separate attack and defense completely from each other but also isolate the way of their application. Indeed, someone can recite the words of Sun Zi's and Wu Zi's *Art of War*, but if they can not understand how to apply them in practice, how can they get to know the mysterious subtleties of the unity of attack and defense?"

Tang Taizong said: "*The Methods of the 'Sima'* states that 'even though a state is big, it will definitely perish if it loves war' and that 'even though a state is in peace, the peace will be endangered if it is not prepared for war.' Is this also a statement about attack and defense?"

Li Jing said: "If one has a state and family, how could he not discuss attacking and defending? Attacking does not stop with just attacking the enemy's cities and battle formations. It also includes the way to defeat the enemy's strategic

【原文】

攻者，不止攻其城击其阵而已，必有攻其心之术焉。守者，不止完其壁坚其阵而已，必也守吾气而有待焉。大而言之，为君之道；小而言之，为将之法。夫攻其心者，所谓知彼者也；守吾气者，所谓知己者也。”

太宗曰：“诚哉！朕尝临阵，先料敌之心与己之心孰审，然后彼可得而知焉；察敌之气与己之气孰治，然后我可得而知焉。是以知彼知己，兵家大

【今译】

必须有打破敌人战略企图、动摇敌人军心的方法；防守，也不只要有完善的城防、坚固的阵势，还必须保持旺盛的士气，待机破敌。这些攻守之道大而言之，是作为君主应当懂得的道理；小而言之，是作为将领应当掌握的方法。能打破敌人的企图、动摇敌人的军心，就是所谓的知彼；能够保持自己一方旺盛的士气，就是所谓的知己。”

太宗说：“确实是这样。朕每逢临敌对阵，总是先分析敌人的作战企图与我的作战企图，看谁更审慎，然后敌人的企图是否高明就知道了；考察敌

intention and shake the morale of his troops.Neither defending ends with just complete city walls and solid formations. It also involves high spirit and morale and waiting for the opportunity to defeat the enemy. These concepts of attacking and defending, speaking in big terms, are concepts that a ruler should understand, and in small terms, are methods that generals ought to master. To be able to defeat the enemy's strategic intention and shake the enemy troops' morale is the so-called 'knowing the enemy,' and to be able to keep a high spirit of your own troops is the so-called 'knowing yourself'."

Tang Taizong said: "That is true! Whenever I was about to engage the enemy in battle, I would compare the enemy's strategic intention with mine and see whose was more prudent, then I would know whether his intention was wise or not. I would also compare the enemy troops' morale with that of my troops' and see whose morale was higher, then I would know whether we would win. So, 'Knowing the enemy and knowing yourself' is the most important concept for any military strategist. If contemporary generals, even if not able to know the enemy, are

【原文】

要。今之将臣，虽未知彼，苟能知己，则安有失利者哉！”

靖曰：“孙武所谓‘先为不可胜’者，知己者也；‘以待敌之可胜’者，知彼者也。又曰：‘不可胜在己，可胜在敌。’臣斯须不敢失此诫。”

太宗曰：“《孙子》言三军可夺气之法：‘朝气锐，昼气惰，暮气归。善用兵者，避其锐气，击其惰归。’如何？”

靖曰：“夫含生禀血，鼓作斗争，虽死不省者，

【今译】

军的士气与我军的士气谁更旺盛，然后我方能不能取胜就可以知道了。所以知彼知己是兵家最重要的原则。现在的将领，即使不知彼，假如能够做到知己，那么哪会有失利的呢。”

李靖说：“孙武所说的‘先为不可胜’（先要创造条件，使自己不可为敌人所战胜），就是知己；他说的‘以待敌之可胜’（等待敌人出现可以被战胜的机会），这就是知彼。他又说：‘不可胜在己，可胜在敌。’（不可被敌人战胜，主动权在我；能否战胜敌人，要看敌人是否失着）我用兵作战时一刻也不敢违背这一诫语。”

唐太宗说：“《孙子兵法》讲到瓦解敌军士气的方法时说：‘朝气锐，昼气惰，暮气归。善用兵者，避其锐气，击其惰归。’（军队初战时士气饱满，过一段时间就逐渐懈怠，最后士气就衰竭了；所以善于用兵的人，要避开敌人初来时的锐气，等待敌人士气懈怠衰竭时再去打击它）这种说法怎么样？”

李靖说：“一切有生命的东西，为了生存鼓起

able to know themselves, how can they be defeated?"

Li Jing said: "What Sun Wu meant by 'first making yourself unconquerable' is 'knowing yourself,' and what he meant by 'wait until the enemy can be conquered' is 'knowing the enemy.' He also said that 'being unconquerable depends on yourself while being able to win lies with the mistakes made by the enemy.' At battle, I never dared to go against this commandment even for a moment."

Tang Taizong said: "In discussing how to rob the enemy troops of their morale, *Sun Zi's Art of War* says : 'In the morning, the spirit of the enemy is high; during the day, it becomes indolent; at dusk, it may be exhausted. So a clever commander should avoid the enemy when his spirit is high and attack him when his spirit becomes indolent and exhausted.' What do you think of this statement?"

Li Jing said: "All living things would struggle to the end of their lives for their survival with great courage, and it is the spirit that causes them to do so. Thus a good commander must first examine the morale of his troops and encourage

【原文】

气使然也。故用兵之法，必先察吾士众，激吾胜气，乃可以击敌焉。吴起‘四机’，以气机为上，无他道也，能使人人自斗，则其锐莫当。所谓朝气锐者，非限时刻而言也，举一日始末为喻也。凡三鼓而敌不衰不竭，则安能必使之惰归哉？盖学者徒谓(诵)空文，而为敌所诱。苟悟夺之之理，则兵可任矣。”

太宗曰：“卿尝言李勣能兵法，久可用否？然

【今译】

勇气进行斗争，至死也不害怕，这是由于有‘气’使它这样。所以用兵的方法，必须首先考察我军士气的心理，激励起敢打必胜的信念，这样才可去进击敌人。吴起所说‘气机’、‘地机’、‘事机’、‘力机’这‘四机’，是以‘气机’作为首要一条的，没有别的道理，就是说激发每个士兵都有敢打敢拼的精神，那么全军必然锐不可当。所谓‘朝气锐’，并不是专指一日当中某个特定的时间说的，而是举一天中的开始与结束作比喻。已经激战过了‘三鼓’，而敌人士气仍然能不衰不竭，那又怎么能说敌人一定是士气衰竭的呢？学习兵法的人，只知道白白背诵兵书上的条文，结果在实战中被敌人诱骗了。假如能领悟剥夺敌军士气的道理，就可以把兵交给他去指挥。”

唐太宗说：“你曾经说李勣懂得兵法，天长日久还可以任用他吗？如果不是我亲自驾驭控制他，

them to fight and to win, and then let them attack the enemy. Wu Qi discussed four vital points—the point of morale, of terrain, of stratagem and of capacity. Of the four, the point of morale is the foremost. There is no other way. If you can raise the morale of all the soldiers and make them eager to fight, then the whole army will become irresistible. When Sun Zi said 'in the morning, the spirit of the enemy is high,' he did not refer to certain hours of the day but used the beginning and end of the day as an analogy. If in a fierce battle, the drum has been sounded three times and the enemy's spirit has neither declined nor become depleted, then how can you say that the enemy's morale has declined? Those who study the art of war only know to recite the words and text of military books; as a result, they would be misled by the enemy in the war. If one could understand the way to rob the enemy of his morale, then you can entrust the army to him."

Tang Taizong said: "You once said that Li Ji knew military strategy, but can he be used from a long-term point of view? If I am no longer around to direct and control him in person, he

【原文】

非朕控御，则不可用也，他日太子治若何御之？”

靖曰：“为陛下计，莫若黜勣，令太子复用之，则必感恩图报，于理何损乎？”

太宗曰：“善！朕无疑矣。”

太宗曰：“李勣若与长孙无忌共掌国政，他日如何？”

靖曰：“勣，忠义臣，可保任也。无忌佐命大功，陛下以肺腹之亲，委之辅相，然外貌下士，内实嫉贤。故尉迟敬德面折其短，遂引退焉；侯君集

【今译】

恐怕就不好使用了。将来太子李治继位后，怎么控制他呢？”

李靖说：“为陛下打算，不如由您免去李勣的职务，将来再由太子起用他，那么他一定会感恩图报，这在情理上有什么妨碍呢？”

太宗说：“好，朕没什么疑虑了。”

太宗说：“李勣如果和长孙无忌共同掌管国家大事，将来会怎样呢？”

李靖说：“李勣是忠义纯臣，可以保证他能胜任。长孙无忌有辅佐陛下创业的大功，陛下又以肺腑至亲委任他做宰相。但此人外表上礼贤下士，其实内心嫉贤妒能。所以，尉迟敬德曾当面指责他的短处，以致辞官隐退；侯君集恨他忘掉旧情，以致

might not be used as such. In the future, when Crown Prince Li Zhi succeeds to the throne, how can he be controlled?"

Li Jing said: "To plan on behalf of Your Majesty, I would suggest that you dismiss Li Ji and have the prince to reemploy him later. Then he will certainly feel grateful and think of repaying it. Does it not stand to reason?"

Tang Taizong said: "Good. I have no doubts about it then."

Tang Taizong said: "If I have Li Ji and Zhangsun Wuji govern the state together, what do you think will happen in the future?"

Li Jing said: "Li Ji is a loyal and righteous court official and I can guarantee that he is competent for that. Zhangsun Wuji made great contributions in assisting Your Majesty to found the imperial court and Your Majesty in a very friendly and sincere way appointed him as the prime minister. However, although this man appears to be very courteous to the wise and respectful to the learned, he is actually quite jealous of the Worthies. Thus Yuchi Jingde raked up his shortcomings and had to retire; Hou Junji hated him for forgetting old friends and as a

【原文】

恨其忘旧，因以犯逆。皆无忌致其然也。陛下询及臣，臣不敢避其说。”

太宗曰：“勿泄也，朕徐思其处置。”

太宗曰：“汉高祖能将将，其后韩、彭见诛，萧何下狱，何故如此？”

靖曰：“臣观刘、项皆非将将之君。当秦之亡也，张良本为韩报仇，陈平、韩信皆怨楚不用，故假汉之势，自为奋尔。至于萧、曹、樊、灌，悉由

【今译】

参与了废立太子的谋反行动而被杀。这都是长孙无忌造成的。陛下询问到我，我不敢避而不谈。”

太宗说：“不要泄露，让我慢慢考虑处置的办法。”

唐太宗说：“人们都说汉高祖刘邦善于统御将帅，可是后来韩信、彭越都被他杀了，萧何也被投入监狱，为什么会弄成这样？”

李靖说：“我看刘邦、项羽都不是善于御将的君主。当秦朝行将灭亡的时候，张良本来是为韩国报仇的，陈平、韩信都因怨恨项羽不重用自己，所以才投奔刘邦，借其声势而为自己的目标奋斗。至于萧何、曹参、樊哙、灌婴，起初都是亡命之徒。

result took part in the conspiracy against the designation of the crown prince and was executed. All these were brought about by Zhangsun Wuji. Since Your Majesty asked me, I dare not avoid talking about it."

Tang Taizong said: "Do not let it leak out. I will think for some time on how to settle it."

Tang Taizong said: "People say that Liu Bang, Emperor Gao Zu of Han, was good at employing and controlling his generals, but later on Han Xin and Peng Yue were both executed by him, and Xiao He was thrown into jail. How could all these happen?"

Li Jing said: "In my opinion, neither Liu Bang nor Xiang Yu was a ruler capable of using and controlling generals. At the time when the Qin Dynasty was about to collapse, Zhang Liang originally wanted to avenge the state of Han, and Chen Ping and Han Xin resented Xiang Yu's failure to employ them so the three of them all went to Liu Bang in order to take advantage of his power and influence to reach their own goals. As for Xiao He, Cao Sen, Fan Kuai and Guan Ying, they were actually people fleeing for their lives. With their help, Liu Bang conquered

【原文】

亡命，高祖因之以得天下。设使六国之后复立，人人各怀其旧，则虽有能将将之才，岂为汉用哉？臣谓汉得天下，由张良借箸之谋，萧何漕挽之功也。以此言之，韩、彭见诛，范增不用，其事同也。臣故谓刘、项皆非将将之君。”

太宗曰：“光武中兴，能保全功臣，不任以吏事，此则善于将将乎？”

靖曰：“光武虽藉前构，易于成功，然莽势不

【今译】

高祖刘邦借助了他们的力量得到天下。假使让六国的后人复位立国，人人都怀念各自的故国旧君，即使刘邦有统御将领的才能，他们又怎么会为刘邦所用呢？我认为刘邦能得天下，是因为得力于张良的借箸之谋和萧何的漕挽之功。就这些事例来说，韩信、彭越被诛，范增不得重用，是同类性质的事。臣所以才说刘邦、项羽都不是善于统御将帅的君主。”

太宗说：“汉光武帝中兴汉室，能够保全功臣，但又不让他们管事。这就是善于统御将帅吧？”

李靖说：“光武帝虽然是借助于前人基业，容易获得成功，然而王莽势力之大不亚于当年的项羽，寇恂、邓禹的才干并不比萧何、张良高明，可是光武帝却能以至诚待人，用柔术治政，保全功臣，这比

All Under Heaven. If the descendants of the Six States had been allowed to reestablish their old states, everyone would have embraced their old states and rulers, then, even if Liu Bang had had the ability to command the generals, how could they have rendered their service to him? So I think that Liu Bang's victory should be attributed to Zhang Liang's plans and strategies and Xiao He's efforts and achievements. From this standpoint, Han Xin and Peng Yue being executed and Fan Zen not being used are the same in nature. Therefore I think that neither Liu Bang nor Xiang Yu was a ruler capable of controlling generals."

Tang Taizong said: "When Emperor Guangwu restored the Han Dynasty, he preserved his meritorious generals but did not entrust them with civil affairs. Is this being capable of controlling generals?"

Li Jing said: "Although Emperor Guangwu easily attained success based on what had been achieved formerly, still Wang Meng was no less powerful than Xiang Yu and Kou Xun and Deng Yu were no less capable than Xiao He and Han Xin. However, Emperor Guangwu was honest to

【原文】

下于项籍，寇、邓未越于萧、张，独能推赤心用柔治保全功臣，贤于高祖远矣！以此论将将之道，臣谓光武得之。”

太宗曰：“古者出师命将，斋三日，授之以钺，曰：‘从此至天，将军制之。’又授之以斧，曰：‘从此至地，将军制之。’又推其毂，曰：‘进退唯时。’既行，军中但闻将军之令，不闻君命。朕谓此

【今译】

汉高祖要高明多了。从这些事情来论统御将帅的方法，我认为光武帝是成功的。”

唐太宗说：“古时候的人出征作战任命大将时，都先斋戒三天，然后举行仪式，把象征权威的钺授予将领，宣布说：‘从这里上至九天，一切事情均由将军裁定。’又把象征生杀之权的斧授予将领，宣布说：‘从这里下至九地，一切事情均由将军裁夺。’又推动将军乘坐的车子说：‘军队的进退由将军根据实际情况全权决断。’军队出发之后，军中的一切事情只听将军的指挥，不再听君主的命令。朕

his subordinates, governed the state with tender policies and preserved his generals. So he was much wiser than Liu Bang. If we discuss the ability to control generals based on this, I would say that Emperor Guangwu was successful."

Tang Taizong said: "In ancient times, when dispatching an army and appointing a commanding general, the ruler would perform a fast of three days and then ritually handed the general a *yue* (an ancient weapon shaped like a broad ax which symbolized authority), pronouncing: 'From here up to the highest of the heavens, everything will be decided by the general.' After that, he would also give the general an ax which symbolized the power to punish and execute, pronouncing: 'From here to the deepest of the earth, everything will be decided by the general.' Then he would push the chariot of the general and say: 'The general will have the total power to decide the advancing and withdrawing of the army in accordance with the situation.' After the army set off, all affairs of the army would be put under the command of the general but not the ruler. I note that these ceremonies have long been abandoned. Now I would like to

【原文】

礼久废，今欲与卿参定遣将之仪，如何？”

靖曰：“臣窃谓圣人制作，致斋于庙者，所以假威于神也；授斧钺又推其毂者，所以委寄以权也。今陛下每有出师，必与公卿议论，告庙而后遣，此则邀以神至矣；每有任将，必使之便宜从事，此则假以权重矣，何与(异)于致斋推毂邪？尽合古礼，其义同焉，不须参定。”

【今译】

以为，这种礼制早已废弃了，现在我想和你一起参照古代的礼制，拟定新的遣将仪式，你看怎么样？”

李靖说：“我认为，古代圣贤君主们制定的在宗庙斋戒的礼仪，是为了假借神灵的威势；授斧钺和推战车，是为了授予出征的将领以军权。现在陛下每次出征，都要先与大臣们商议，并告祭宗庙然后才派遣将帅，这已经做到祈请神明保佑了。每当陛下任命大将时，总是赋予他们临机决断、便宜处事的全权，这就给了他们以权威，这与古代斋戒推毂有什么不同呢？这完全合乎古代的礼仪，意义相同，不必再参照古制重新订立礼仪了。”

discuss with you and work out some new ceremonies for the appointing of the commanding general with reference to the ancient ones. What do you think of it?"

Li Jing said: "In my opinion, ancient wise rulers established the ceremonies to perform fast in temples because they wanted to draw awesomeness from the spirits. They gave the yue and ax to the dispatched general and pushed his chariot because they wanted to grant him the authority to command. Today, whenever Your Majesty is about to send an expedition, you will discuss it with the court officials and hold sacrificial ceremonies at the temple before appointing and sending the generals. This is already an earnest request for the blessing of the spirits. Whenever Your Majesty appoints a general, you always grant him the power to make decisions and take actions on the spot well to their convinience. This, then, is loaning him great authority. How does it differ from observing a fast and pushing the chariot in ancient times? It completely accords with the ancient rites and the meaning is the same. There is no need to establish a new rite after the ancient ones."

【原文】

靖(上)曰："善！"乃命近臣书此二事，为后世法。

太宗曰："阴阳术数，废之可乎？"

靖曰："不可。兵者，诡道也，托之以阴阳术数，则使贪使愚，兹不可废也。"

太宗曰："卿尝言，天官时日，明将不法，暗者拘之。废亦宜然？"

靖曰："昔纣以甲子日亡，武王以甲子日兴。天官时日，甲子一也，殷乱周治，兴亡异焉。又宋武帝以往亡日起兵，军吏以为不可，帝曰：'我往彼亡'，果克之。由此言之，可废明矣。然而田单为

【今译】

李靖说："好。"于是命令近臣把这两件事记载下来，作为后世出兵命将的法度。

唐太宗说："阴阳术数，废掉它可以吗？"

李靖说："不可。用兵作战，讲求诡诈之道。假托阴阳术数，就可以驱使贪婪和愚昧的人，所以不可废除。"

太宗说："你曾经说过，天官时日这一套，明智的将领不去取法它，只有愚昧的将领才拘泥于这一套做法。废掉它也是可以的吧？"

李靖说："从前，商纣王在甲子日那天灭亡，周武王却在甲子日那天成功。按照天官时日，同是甲子这一天，结果是殷乱周兴，兴盛和衰亡截然不同。又比如，南北朝时宋武帝刘裕偏要在术数家认为最不吉利的'往亡日'起兵讨伐南燕，将领们认

Tang Taizong said: "Good." Then he ordered his attending courtier to record the two practices as a norm of appointing and sending generals to be followed by people of later ages.

Tang Taizong said: "Can the practices of Yin and Yang be abandoned?"

Li Jing said: "No, they can not. Deception is important for warfare. With Yin and Yang practices, we can manipulate the greedy and stupid, so they can not be abandoned."

Tang Taizong said: "You once said that selecting astrologically auspicious seasons and days is not the method of a wise general. Only stupid ones stick to that sort of practice. So it should be abandoned."

Li Jing said: "In the past, King Zhou of the Shang Dynasty perished on a day designated as *Jiazi* (Heavenly Stem One and Earthly Branch One in the sixty-year cycle of traditional Chinese chronology) and King Wu of the Zhou Dynasty succeeded on the same day. If one has to observe astrologically auspicious seasons and days, why on the same day of Jiazi should the Shang Dynasty have perished and the Zhou Dynasty flourished? What a great difference! Another example

【原文】

燕所围，单命一人为神，拜而祠之。神言：‘燕可破’，单于是以火牛出击燕，大破之。此是兵家诡道。天官时日，亦由此也。”

太宗曰：“田单托神怪而破燕，太公焚蓍龟而

【今译】

为不可出兵。宋武帝说：‘我去进攻，他们灭亡。’果然大败南燕，攻克广固城。由此说来，阴阳术数、天官时日之类的东西可以废除是很明显的了。然而，齐将田单被燕军围困于即墨的时候，命令一个士卒假扮神师，装神弄鬼，并把他供奉起来。这个装神的士兵说：‘燕军可以打败。’于是，田单用火牛阵出击，大败燕军。这就是军事上的诡诈之道。天官时日也是如同这一类的事情。”

太宗说：“田单假托神怪，结果大败燕军；太公吕望烧掉了用来占卜的蓍草和龟甲，结果灭掉商

is when Liu Yu, Emperor Wu Di of Song of the Northern and Southern Dynasties, was about to go on an expedition against the state of Southern Yan, the day he chose to set off was a day considered by the *Yin* and *Yang* diviners as an ominous 'going to perish day.' All his generals thought he should not set off on that day, but the Emperor said: 'I will attack and they will perish.' Indeed, he defeated the state of Southern Yan and took the city of Guang Gu. From these cases, we can say that it is clear that such things as Yin and Yang practices and selection of astrologically auspicious seasons and days can be abandoned. However, when Tian Dan, the general of the state of Qi, was besieged in Ji Mo by the army of Yan, he ordered a soldier to disguise himself as a spirit and enshrined and worshiped him. This disguised soldier said: 'The army of Yan can be defeated.' Then Tian Dan launched an attack with flaming oxen and completely defeated the army of Yan. This is military deception. The selection of astrologically auspicious seasons and days is similar to this."

Tang Taizong said: "Tian Shan resorted to

【原文】

灭纣，二事相反，何也？”

靖曰：“其机一也，或逆而取之，或顺而行之是也。昔太公佐武王，至牧野遇雷雨，旗鼓毁折，散宜生欲卜吉而后行，此则因军中疑惧，必假卜以问神焉。太公以谓腐草枯骨无足问，且以臣伐君，岂可再乎？然观散宜生发机于前，太公成机于后，

【今译】

纣。这两件事在做法上截然相反，结果却一样，为什么呢？”

李靖说：“他们在善于抓住事情的契机、稳定军心上是一致的。一个是从破除迷信的角度采取的方法，一个是从利用迷信的角度采取的方法。当年姜太公辅佐周武王讨伐商纣进军至牧野，遇上雷雨天气，旗鼓都被击毁折断。散宜生提出先占卜一下凶吉再采取行动。这是因为军中对雷雨毁坏旗鼓感到疑惑恐惧，所以必须假借占卜问神来安定军心。姜太公认为占卜用的腐草枯骨不值一问，更何况周武王以臣子身份讨伐君主，这样的军事行动怎么可以等待吉日再行举事呢？然而，看起来先是散宜生故意提出需要占卜的问题，然后是姜太公见机行事否定了占卜，虽然他们的做法完全不一样，但稳定

spiris and ghosts and defeated Yan while Taigong burned the yarrows and tortoise shells for divination and exterminated Zhou of Shang. These two affairs are contradictory to each other, but the results are the same. Why?"

Li Jing said: "They are alike in grasping the opportunities and keeping the troops unruffled with one doing away with superstition and one taking advantage of superstition. In antiquity, Jiang Taigong assisted King Wu of Zhou on an expedition against Zhou of Shang, they reached Mu Ye where they went into a thunderstorm and the flags and drums were either broken or destroyed. San Yisheng made a suggestion to divine first before taking any actions. He felt that because of the doubts and fear within the army, they must rely on divination and the help of spirits to calm the troops. But Taiogong thought that the rotted grass and dry bones for divination were not worth asking. Moreover, as in this case where King Wu of Zhou was on an expedition as a subordinate against his ruler, how could people wait for an auspicious day to conduct such an operation? In this case, however, it appears that San Yisheng's suggestion of divination at the

【原文】

逆顺虽异，其理致则同。臣前所谓术数不可废者，盖存其机于未萌也，及其(成)功，在人事而已。”

太宗曰：“当今将帅，唯李勣、道宗、薛万彻，除道宗以亲属外，孰堪大用？”

靖曰：“陛下尝言勣、道宗用兵，不大胜亦不大败；万彻若不大胜，即须大败。臣愚思圣言，不求大胜亦不大败者，节制之兵也；或大胜或大败者，

【今译】

军心的动机却是一致的。我前边说过阴阳术数不可废弃，那是在事情还没有露出苗头的时候，利用它来控制人们的心理。至于一切事情的成功，还是取决于人的努力。”

唐太宗说：“现在的将帅，在李勣、李道宗、薛万彻三人中，除了道宗是亲属之外，谁还可以重用呢？”

李靖说：“陛下曾经说，李勣、道宗用兵打仗不能取得特大的胜利，也不会遭到重大失败；薛万彻用兵如果不是获得大胜就是遭到大败。我想到圣上曾经这么说：不求大胜也不遭大败的军队，是训练有素的军队；要么大胜要么大败的军队，是侥幸能取得成功的军队。所以孙武说：‘善战者，立于

beginning and Jiang Taigong's negation of the suggestion subsequently were contrary one to the other, but their motives were the same—to keep the troops unruffled. When I previously stated that the Yin and Yang practices should not be abandoned, it was meant that these practices could be used for psychological control over our men before things have begun to manifest themselves. But whether one will be successful or not depends on his own efforts."

Tang Taizong said: "Of the three generals of Li Ji, Li Daozong and Xue Wanche at present, apart from Daozong who is a relative, who can be entrusted with great responsibility?"

Li Jing said: "Your Majesty once said that when fighting a war Li Ji and Daozong would not achieve great victories, but nor would they suffer disastrous defeats; while Xue Wanche would either achieve great victories or suffer disastrous defeats. I remember that Your Majesty once said that an army which does not strive for great victories but nor will suffer disastrous defeats is a well-trained army; while an army which may achieve great victories but also may suffer disastrous defeats is an army relying

【原文】

幸而成功者也。故孙武云：‘善战者，立于不败之地，而不失敌之败也。’节制在我云尔。”

太宗曰：“两阵相临，欲言不战，安可得乎？”

靖曰：“昔晋(秦)师伐秦(晋)，交绥而退。《司马法》曰：‘逐奔不远，纵绥不及。’臣谓绥者，御辔之索也。我兵既有节制，彼敌亦正行伍，岂敢轻战哉？故有出而交绥，退而不逐，各防其失败者也。孙武云：‘勿击堂堂之阵，无邀正正之旗。’若

【今译】

不败之地，而不失敌之败也。’(善于打仗的人，总是使自己立于不败之地，而不放过击败敌人的机会)这说明对部队能否指挥控制得住，完全在于自己。”

唐太宗说：“两军对阵，如果不想交战，怎样才能办到？”

李靖说：“从前秦国军队讨伐晋国，双方刚一接触就退兵不战了。《司马法》说：‘逐奔不远，纵绥不及。’(追逐败北的军队不能追得太远，急行军不要超过一定的限度)臣认为‘绥’就是驾御马匹的缰绳。我军的行动既是训练有素很有节制，敌

on good fortune to be successful. Thus Sun Wu said: 'A wise commander always ensures that his forces are put in an invincible position, and at the same time will be sure to miss no opportunity to defeat the enemy.' This tells that whether you can have a good control and command over your troops depends only on yourself."

Tang Taizong said: "When two armies approach each other, if we do not want to fight, how can we manage it?"

Li Jing said: "In antiquity, when the army of the state of Jin and the army of the state of Qin were at war, both of them withdrew the moment they approached each other. *The Methods of the "Sima"* says: 'Do not pursue a fleeing army too far and give a free Shui only to acertain extent.' I think that Shui here refers to the reins of a horse. If our army is well -trained and controlled, and the enemy's formation is well-organized, can you imagine that either one would run rashly into a battle? That is why they met and then withdrew with neither of them pursuing. They just wanted to defend themselves from being defeated. Sun Wu said: 'Desist from attacking an army whose formations are in an impressive

【原文】

两阵体均势等，苟一轻肆，为其所乘，则或大败，理使然也。是故兵有不战，有必战；夫不战者在我，必战者在敌。”

太宗曰：“不战在我，何谓也？”

靖曰：“孙武云：‘我不欲战者，画地而守之，敌不得与我战者，乖其所之也。’敌有人焉，则交绥之间未可图也。故曰：不战在我。夫必战在敌者，孙武云：‘善动敌者，形之，敌必从之；予之，敌

【今译】

方的队形也是阵容严整，这样怎么敢轻易交战呢？所以才会有临战而退、退而不追的情况，都是为了防止失败。孙武说：‘勿击堂堂之阵，无邀正正之旗。’（不要去攻击阵容堂皇实力强大的敌人，不要去拦击旗帜整齐部署周密的敌人）如果敌我双方势均力敌，一旦轻举妄动，为敌所乘，就会招致大败，这是很自然的道理。所以用兵作战，有时不能打，有时则必须打。不打是由于我没有必胜的把握；必须打是因为敌人有可乘之隙。”

太宗说：“不打是由于我没有必胜的把握，这是指什么说的？”

李靖说：“孙武说：‘我不欲战者，画地而守之，敌不得与我战者，乖其所之也。’（我军不想打，虽然画地防守，敌人也无法来同我作战，是因为我使敌人改变了进攻的方向）敌人阵营中有深谙兵法的人，那么在两军交战时，我方未必能够取胜。

array, and refrain from intercepting an enemy whose banners are in perfect order.' When we and the enemy are equal in strength, should we move rashly, we will give the enemy an opportunity and suffer a disastrous defeat. This is common sense. So, at war, sometimes you must fight, sometimes you must not. You must not fight because you do not have the confidence to win, while you must fight because the enemy has created some advantages for you to take."

Tang Taizong said: "What do you mean by 'you must not fight because you do not have the confidence to win'?"

Li Jing said: "Sun Wu said: 'If we do not wish to fight, we can prevent the enemy from engaging us even though the lines of our encampment can be traced out on the ground. This is because we divert him from going where he wishes.' If the enemy has someone who excels at military tactics and strategy, then we may not be able to win the battle when engaging the enemy. So, we do not fight because we can not meet the requirements for a victory and we must fight because the enemy has created some advantages for us to take. Sun Wu said: 'One who is adept

【原文】

必取之；以利动之，以本待之。’敌无人焉，则必来战，吾得以乘而破之。故曰：必战者在敌。”

太宗曰：“深乎，节制之兵！得其法则昌，失其法则亡。卿为纂述历代善于节制者，具图来上，朕当择其精微，垂于后世。”

靖曰：“臣前所进黄帝、太公二阵图，并《司马法》、诸葛亮奇正之法，此已精悉。历代名将，用

【今译】

所以说不与敌人决战，是因为我取胜的条件不具备。当必须打时是因为敌人有机可乘，孙武说：‘善动敌者，形之，敌必从之；予之，敌必取之；以利动之，以本待之。’（善于调动敌人的将帅，伪装假象迷惑敌人，敌人就会听从调动；用小利引诱敌人，敌人就会来夺取。用这样的办法去调动敌人，用重兵来伺机掩击敌人）敌人阵营中没有谙熟兵法的人，那么就会轻率出战，我便可以乘隙击破敌人。所以说，必须与敌人作战，是由于敌人有机可乘。”

太宗说：“有关节制之兵的道理很深奥啊！掌握了这个法则就会昌盛，违背了这个法则就会灭亡。你要把历代善于节制用兵的将领事迹汇编起来，编制成图呈上，朕要选择其中道理深刻的部分，让它留传于后世。”

李靖说：“臣以前呈上的黄帝、太公二种阵图，以及《司马法》、诸葛亮论述奇正的兵法，已经很详尽精细了。历代名将中只运用其中一两条道理而成功的大有人在。但是撰写史书的人里很少有懂军事

at keeping the enemy on the move maintains deceitful appearances, according to which the enemy will act. He lures with something that the enemy is certain to take. By so doing he keeps the enemy on the move and then waits for the right moment to make a sudden ambush with picked troops.' If the enemy does not have anyone who excels at military tactics and strategy, he will rashly come forth to fight, and then we can take the opportunity and defeat him."

Tang Taizong said: "This concept about a well-disciplined army is very profound! One will flourish going with this concept and perish going against it. You should compile the deeds of the generals throughout all times who excelled at constraining the army and present them to me with diagrams. I will select the quintessential ones and have them passed to later ages."

Li Jing said: "The two diagrams of the Yellow Emperor's and Taigong's dispositions together with *The Methods of the "Sima"* and Zhuge Liang's strategies for unorthodox and orthodox which I submitted previously are already very highly detailed. There were many who, among the famous generals in history, employed

【原文】

其一二而成功者亦众矣。但史官鲜克知兵，不能纪其实迹焉。臣敢不奉诏，当纂述以闻。”

太宗曰：“兵法孰为最深者？”

靖曰：“臣尝分为三等，使学者当渐而至焉。一曰道，二曰天地，三曰将法。夫道之说，至微至深，《易》所谓‘聪明睿智神武而不杀’者是也。夫天之说阴阳，地之说险易。善用兵者，能以阴夺

【今译】

的，不能纪录下这方面的史实事迹。臣哪里敢不执行您的诏命，一定要把有关的史实编撰成书上报。”

唐太宗说：“古代兵法中哪一家最为精深？”

李靖说：“我曾经把兵法分成三等，让学习的人可以循序渐进。一是‘道’，二是‘天地’，三是‘将法’。所谓‘道’是最微妙最深刻的理论，也就是《易》中所说的‘聪明、睿智、神武而不杀’(无所不闻、无所不见、无所不通、无所不知，变化莫测，戡定祸乱，以德不以刑威而定天下）的那种最高智慧。所谓‘天’，是指阴阳寒暑；所谓‘地’，是指远近险易。善于用兵的将领，能够以阴柔克服

only one or two of them and achieved success. But among those who wrote or complied history books, there were very few who understood military affairs, so they were unable to keep a record of this kind of achievements. How dare I disobey your imperial instruction? You can be sure that I will compile all the concerned historical records into a book and submit it to you."

Tang Taizong said: "Which is the most important of the ancient schools of art of war?"

Li Jing said: "I once divided the art of war into three levels to allow the learners to proceed in an orderly and gradual way. The first is '*Dao*,' the second is 'Heaven and Earth' and the third is 'Methods of Generalship.' '*Dao*' is the most profound and subtle concept. It is what *The Book of Changes* refers to as the greatest wisdom of 'all-perceiving, all-knowing, always changing and pacifying All Under Heaven with virtue instead of punishments and awesomeness.' The 'Heaven' refers to *Yin* and *Yang* and winter and summer; and the 'Earth' refers to far and near and difficult and easy. A good commanding general is able to overcome the masculine roughness with feminine tenderness and turn difficulty

【原文】

阳，以险攻易，孟子所谓'天时地利'者是也。夫将法之说，在乎任人利器，《三略》所谓'得士者昌'，管仲所谓'器必坚利'者是也。"

太宗曰："然。吾谓不战而屈人之兵者上也，百战百胜者中也，深沟高垒以自守者下也。以是较量，孙武著书，三等皆具焉。"

靖曰："观其文，迹其事，亦可差别矣。若张良、范蠡、孙武，脱然高引，不知所往，此非知道，安能尔乎？若乐毅、管仲、诸葛亮，战必胜，守必

【今译】

阳刚，以险要夺取平易。这就是孟子所说上顺天时、下适地利。所谓'将'，主要在于选拔人才、完善武器装备，《三略》说的得到贤士者昌盛，管仲说的装备器具必须坚固锋利，就是关于这方面的道理。"

太宗说："是啊。我认为不用交战就能挫败敌人的，是最高层次；百战百胜的，是中等层次；深沟高垒善于防守的，是下等层次。用这个标准去衡量，孙武的军事著作里，三等都讲到了。"

李靖说："研究古人的述著，考察古人的事迹，也可以看出古人的差别来。比如张良、范蠡、孙武功成之后急流勇退、飘然归隐，不知去向。如果这不是深谙'道'说，怎么能做得到呢？比如乐毅、管仲、诸葛亮，他们在用兵上战必胜、守必固，如

into easiness. This is what Mencius referred to as 'takeing advantage of good timing and geographic convenience.' As for the 'Generalship,' it refers to the selection of men and preparation of weapons as said in the *Three Strategems* that one who gains the worthies will prosper, and by Guan Zhong that weapons and equipment must be solid and sharp."

Tang Taizong said: "Yes. I think that one who can subdue the enemy without fighting belongs to the highest level; one who is ever-victorious belongs to the medium level; and one who uses deep moats and high fortifications to defend himself belongs to the lowest. If we take this as a standard, then we can see that all three levels have been discussed in Sun Wu's military writings."

Li Jing said: "When we scrutinize the writings and undertakings of ancients, we can also see the difference among them. For example, Zhang Liang, Fan Li and Sun Wu aqll retired at the height of their career and withdrew into lofty seclusion. No one knew where they had gone. If they had not comprehended the '*Dao*' thoroughly, how could they have done it? Next example would be Yue Yi, Guan Zhong, and

【原文】

固，此非察天时地利，安能尔乎？其次，王猛之保秦，谢安之守晋，非任将择才，缮完自固，安能尔乎？故习兵之学，必先由下以及中，由中以及上，则渐而深矣。不然，则垂空言，徒记诵，无足取也。”

太宗曰：“道家忌三世为将者，不可妄传也，不可不传也，卿其慎之！”

靖再拜出，尽传其书与李勣。

【今译】

果不是明察天时地利，怎么能做得到呢？其次，如王猛安定前秦、谢安捍卫东晋，如果不是恰当地任用将领选择人才，完善防御以求自固，怎么能做得到呢？所以，学习兵法，必须先从下等到中等，再从中等到上等，如此便能由浅入深了。不这样，只会空谈，死记硬背，是不足取的。”

太宗说：“道家的学说，忌讳三代为将，是说兵法不可妄传，但也不可不传。你应当慎重传授。”

李靖再拜而出，将他的全部兵书传授给李勣。

Zhuge Liang. They were always victorious in battle and solid in defense. If they had not been well aware of good timing and geographical convenience, how could they have succeeded? Another example would be Wang Meng's preservation of Former Qin and Xie An's defense of Eastern Jin. If they had not employed right generals and selected talented men, and if they had not improved and solidified their defenses, how could they have managed that? So, to learn military strategies, one must proceed first from the lowest level to the medium level, and then from the medium to the highest, thus going from simple to profound. If not, he will rely on empty words, merely remembering and reciting them. This is not the way to learn."

Tang Taizong said: "According to the doctrine of *Dao*, no general should be appointed in the same family for three successive generations. What it means is that military strategies should not be taught and passed on carelessly, though they have to be taught and passed on. You should be careful when passing them on."

Li Jing bowed again and went out, and turned all his military books over to Li Ji.

图书在版编目(CIP)数据

黄石公三略　唐太宗李卫公问对/黄朴民　萧大维校释;何小东译 .—北京:军事科学出版社,2004.11

(大中华文库)

ISBN 7-80137-720-6

Ⅰ.黄… Ⅱ.①黄… ②萧… ③何… Ⅲ.兵法-中国-汉代-汉、英 Ⅳ.E892.34

中国版本图书馆 CIP 数据核字(2004)第 121791 号

责任编辑:潘宏　王显臣
审　　校:马欣来　梁良兴

大中华文库
黄石公三略　唐太宗李卫公问对
何小东　译

出版者:
军事科学出版社
(北京市海淀区青龙桥军事科学出版社　邮政编码:100091)

制版、排版者:
恒基佳业科技有限公司(北京市海淀区)

印制者:深圳市佳信达印务有限公司

开本:960×640　1/16(精装)　印张:18.75　印数:1-3000 册
2005 年第 1 版第 1 次印刷
(汉英对照)ISBN 7-80137-720-6 /E·485
定价:35.00 元